JERSEY

Secrets of the Sea

Paul Darroch

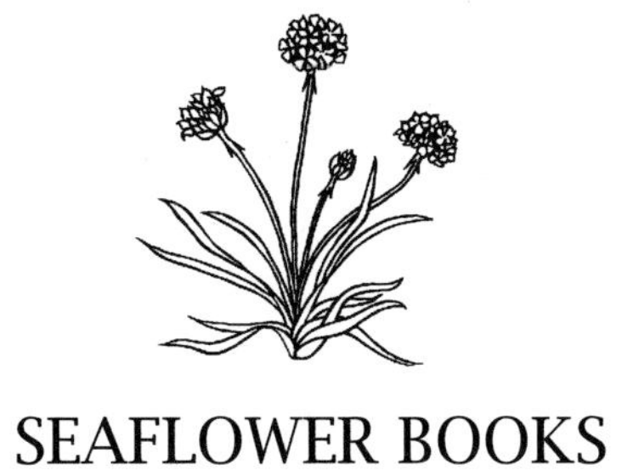

SEAFLOWER BOOKS

Published in 2019 and reprinted in 2020 by
SEAFLOWER BOOKS

www.ex-librisbooks.co.uk

Origination by Seaflower Books

Printed and bound by CPI Group (UK) Ltd
Croydon, CR0 4YY

ISBN 978-1-912020-93-5

Dedicated to I, J and K
In loving memory of Ronald and Joan

Front cover: SS Amazon *on Fire in the Bay of Biscay (1852)*
by Philip John Ouless (1817-1885)
Courtesy of the Jersey Heritage Collections

Contents

Author's Preface   4

Prelude: The White Ship – The Butcher's Story   5

SPRING: AGE OF LEGENDS
   Jersey's Atlantis: The Lost Manor of La Brecquette   13
   Wreckers of Winter Night   16
   The Legend of the Golden Chair   20

SUMMER: AGE OF ADVENTURE
   To the Promised Land: De Carteret's Settling of Sark   24
   Under the Line: Raleigh's Last Voyage   30
   Charles Robin: The Fisher King   36
   The Battle of the Oyster Shells: A Gorey Story   41

AUTUMN: AGE OF PLENTY
   Inside the Fairy Palace: The Great Exhibition   48
   Louisa's Story: Into the Night   54
   Lilian's Story: Into the Heart of China   62
   Elinor Glyn: Jersey's Queen of Hollywood   68

WINTER: AGE OF WAR
   White Star, Blue Iceberg: The *Titanic* Story   82
   T.B. Davis: The World beyond the Wall   94
   Red Letter Day: Sailing for War   107

Epilogue: Flight of the *Ragamuffin*   119

Acknowledgements   125

About the Author   125

Author's Preface

I started to discover Jersey's secrets of the sea on a dark October evening, as blustery weather rolled in from the west. Since the publication of *Jersey: The Hidden Histories*, I had been searching for a compelling theme to bind together my second book. Then I chanced upon the story of the lost manor of La Brecquette, and it abruptly gripped my imagination. Somewhere in the bay beyond, the tide was rising.

On a night such as this, long ago, the sea cleaved the land bridge that tethered us to the continent, and this Island was born. In the ages to come, it would be peopled, settled and invaded, and it would be given a new name. From the very beginning, Jersey's story has been sculpted by the sea.

I imagined Jersey's maritime history unfolding in four distinct seasons. In Jersey's medieval springtime, as it emerged from the fog of myth, the ocean was feared as a primal, destructive force. Local legends tell not only of the waves that drowned La Brecquette, but of the sea wreaking violent retribution on wrongdoers.

As summer dawned, and the Renaissance gave way to the Enlightenment, the old world's horizons tumbled, and adventure called. In this great age of discovery, the mariners of Jersey, from Governor Sir Walter Raleigh to the fisher king Charles Robin, set out to claim the world.

Jersey sailed on into its golden autumn of plenty, the heyday of the Victorian and Edwardian eras. Its restless children would cross the oceans to pursue missionary calling in China, find fame in early Hollywood and build a fortune in Africa.

Jersey seafarers were afforded a ringside seat at some of the defining moments of maritime history. In these pages, we will step onto the bridge of RMS *Titanic* with the Quartermaster from St Ouen, as a Jersey millionairess slumbers in her first-class suite below, and the blue iceberg glints ahead of them in the darkness.

Finally, winter fell hard upon Jersey; an age of suffering and war; of troop-ships leaving for the Western Front, and of a lone boatman escaping the shadow of the Occupation. The cycle of the seasons had come full circle.

All those tales are yet to come. Our story begins on an icy medieval night, aboard a ship of princes. They say it is the most exquisite vessel in the world, and it carries the heir to the throne. Before the hourglass empties, it will lie beneath the waves.

Paul Darroch
Jersey, 2019

PRELUDE

The White Ship: The Butcher's Story

The English Channel
25th November 1120

A ship is gliding home in the winter night. It is bleached as white as bones, and tonight it bears the sons of a King. This is no ordinary vessel. The White Ship dances over the waves, drawn by some unearthly power.

I have never beheld a ship so fair. Each deck is draped in rich gold and plumped with purple cushions. Even the benches are inlaid with jewels. The *Blanche-Nef*, the sailors reverently call it, seemingly speaking of a living thing. The ship is exquisitely sculpted as if from delicate ice, as sleek a craft as ever graced the seas. The elegance that surrounds us is astonishing. Even up here on the chilly main deck, where I am required to loiter as a common tradesman, I see the slender timbers of the poop curving like the gleaming ribs of a prize ox.

*   *   *

I truly know of what I speak, for I am Berold of Rouen, master butcher by trade. I cut up tripe for a living, rip out pigs' bellies and carve up the choicest meats for my Duke's household. I have travelled all the way up here from the great city, where I ply my trade in the shadow of the old Viking cathedral. The lords on this ship spent all too freely at my butcher's bench last month, taking a dozen deliveries of my prime cuts, yet they have left me treacherously short-changed. This is my last chance to claim my debts before these noblemen slip away like eels, back to their conquered kingdom, and leave me a pauper.

I am painfully aware of my humble standing at this fine gathering: I must easily be the poorest man on this ship of kings. I can sense the silent sneers of these princelings in their finery. "Who is this mere commoner in our midst?", they leer. But I have eight mouths to feed at home and will stand my ground. I am come to claim my coin.

The lords seem in no mood to parley with me. Prince William, the firstborn heir, has given orders to break out three immense barrels of wine for all and sundry. The young noblemen have given their enthusiastic assent to the royal command, and all have been drinking deep for hours. Even the detachment of common marines that guard them are like angry geese, set on hissing and squabbling their way back to England. Three hundred befuddled men and women are crammed aboard, each one carousing and giggling as if the world is going to end tonight, and the Lord's appearing is imminent. It hardly seems the best moment to seek my promised payment, but perhaps the intoxication will loosen their purses.

They say the King's own ship left hours ago. He had been offered the service of the *Blanche-Nef* himself. Shipmaster Thomas's father had ferried William the Conqueror to victory at Hastings; would it not be natural for his son to travel as his guest? Yet Henry I, our Duke of Normandy and King of England, refused the offer. He would travel alone. Some curious instinct, some moment of hesitation caused him to pull back, but instead he permitted this strange and beautiful ship to transport his children home.

William, the prince and heir to England and Normandy, carries the royal banner on our ship tonight. He is in the prime of his youth and power, waxing strong. As if in his honour, the water is unusually high tonight, and the waves are almost lapping over the top of the quay.

The priests of Barfleur harbour have come to bless us now, bearing vials of holy water. A sea voyage to England is a perilous exploit at the best of times, but in the depths of winter, when the darkness enfolds the sea, we rely on the mercy of the saints more than ever. Yet I gasp at the scene that passes before my eyes.

The mariners are drunk, and they are mocking and chiding the priests. They are laughing and spitting at the men of God and driving them away like cattle. The proffered blessing is spurned. Scorned and humiliated, the priests scuttle back to the shore. I have never seen a moment of ungodly defiance like it.

Some of the passengers are astounded at this flagrant denial of holy law and want no more of this farce. Some of the great men of Court are leaving the ship. Count Stephen of Mortain, William de Roumare and Edward Salisbury file off the gangplank onto the quay. I too am sick of this buffoonery. As soon as my rightful coin is mine, I will be straight back in that Barfleur inn with a fat pint of cider.

At last I catch the eye of my principal debtor, that flabby lord from Winchester who ordered my choicest cuts and evaded payment. I hasten up to badger him, to assay him with my practiced mix of honeyed words and veiled threats until I am paid in full.

Yet just before I can reach him, the ship lurches forwards. Without cry or warning, we have launched. I am almost pushed to the deck, and as I steady myself, I realise

I have missed my chance. This is more than a tragedy; I am now hurtling across the sea towards the truculent, subjugated realm of England. The return passage alone will lose me a second fortune. I can only watch in shock as the little quay at Barfleur falls away behind me, and the cottages and holy church vanish from sight. Dusk has fallen early, far too early. It is a black and starless night.

On the White Ship, things are falling into anarchy. Chaos has set up court on the ship tonight. All around me, the merriment is undimmed, the revelry is mounting. Serving maids and princelings are openly cavorting, all of them downing the finest wine of Burgundy. The boat is fast becoming an orgy.

Captain Thomas stands proud on the deck, boasting that he owns the night, that he can skip the Channel like a millpond, that this is the fastest ship that the world has ever seen. Young Prince William has drunk deep himself, and is screaming for the race, mad for the chase. "Faster!", the Lord's anointed heir cries. "Let us beat our royal father across this scrap of water that divides us." Then the ship plunges on deeper into the vastness of the Channel.

I seem to be the only one alarmed by this turn of events. The ship seems bereft of old salts, or trained navigators. Instead the young oarsmen, as pissed as newts, are pummelling the sea with the false strength that only wine can bestow. They are flying fast into the night like a blinded falcon.

The boat gathers pace and is skimming like a pebble over the waters. I realise I am trapped on a ship of fools. We are gliding over the waves now at tremendous, unearthly speed, like a galloping seahorse, racing into a void as black as pitch. I curse under my breath. This cannot end well.

Then the world of the living ends. Without a whisper, the string is pulled and the cleaver swings down in the slaughterhouse. Later they would name the culprit as the Raz de Cateville, a black rock curved like a meathook. They say it pierces the sky at low tide, but at highwater it crouches like a beast in waiting, submerged by the waves, waiting for its prey.

Like everyone else, I am thrown upon the deck as the White Ship cleanly shears itself upon the razor. All around me, the ship is splintering into pieces like a toy. The hull has split clean in two; all those delicate white timbers have become matchwood. Down I am plunged, down into this whirlpool of maimed drunks, of shattered wood and fine robes, all falling into the night.

My chest explodes with shock and rage, and I am almost struck unconscious by the sheer weight of the murderous cold. Is this death? Then my racing breath suddenly calms, and I feel a strange clarity. There are shrieks all around me in the night, for God, for help, for their lost loves. In the blackness of the waves the lord and the peasant are equal before their Maker. Or perhaps the tables are turned. For few of these arrogant lords will be able to swim.

Yet for a butcher's son, larking every day in the Seine as a boy, the sea itself holds no terror. It is bitterly, ravishingly cold but I know well enough how to kick and float. I pride myself on my strength and can see the ship's yardarm is close at hand, perched above the waves. Whilst other men flail and drown, I swim with a grim determination towards it, and with a violent heave, I drag myself up and onto it. The ship's hull must be lodged on the seabed, given the shallowness of the reef. So as long as the yardarm holds firm, I will not drown. Another man spies my example and does likewise. We are both clean out of the water, and in my heavy, dripping sheepskin I lie prone and wait in the night.

In the writhing waters beneath me, I watch the tragedy enter its final act. Loyal to the last, two marines have pushed Prince William into the safety of the ship's little skiff, and they start to row him towards the shore. But his sister Matilda is still there in the water, screaming like a dying swan. His heart torn, I hear the Prince order the craft to be turned around, in order to save her. Yet no sooner does he approach than a brace of drowning men hurl themselves at the skiff, desperate to save themselves at any cost. The skiff cleanly flips on its head, capsized. Before my eyes, I see the Lord's anointed snuffed out like a candle in the deep. Prince William Adelin, anointed heir to both Normandy and England, is gone.

Moments later, the arrogant snout of Captain Thomas, clinging to a scrap of driftwood, pokes up somewhere above the brine. "What has become of the king's son?", he asks. "He's gone," I cry out. "He is perished – and all of them with him."

The fool yells back: "Then it is misery for me to live any longer", and he plunges hard into the deep. He knew that his King would be consumed by a fierce and terrible rage; his only choice was between a lingering, painful death in the dungeons of the White Tower or a swift and icy one beneath the waves.

All the cries have fallen silent now, as the ice-breath of the sea stops their mouths and the alchemy of water turns living bodies into frozen corpses. Mockingly, the stars are coming out now, gleaming beautifully so far above the tragedy, like the holy angels of God. I can only see the wreckage of kings floating beneath me.

In my predicament, I resort to prayer. I cry out to Saint Romain, our patron saint of Rouen, to the Holy Mother, to the Lord Jesus Himself for his mercy. But I am not here alone, for another man hangs with me over the deep. Throughout the dark watches of the night we cling together to the yardarm, our teeth chattering above the brine. He is a nobleman, Geoffrey, the son of Gilbert de l'Aigle. He is too slight for all of this, born to a castle fair and a pampered life. But there he clings with me at the end of all things.

The night is dark and full of pain. My back is tortured, as if on a rack. My hands are numb, as bloated as a leper's. My companion Gilbert seems a mere skeleton now, whipped by the wind. I urge him to stay strong, but his spirit has broken. He whispers a final pitiful farewell, commends me to the hands of God, and then he falls down into the deep. I hear a final gasp from the darkness, as he slips into his icy tomb. I have known him only hours, but my heart wails at the loss. My heavy sheepskin is a cloak of snow around me, and the wind scourges me through it. Even with my butcher's strength, I will not be able to hold on much longer. I look up to heaven. Venus, the morning star, is hanging there, a witness and judge over us all.

Dawn is breaking at last now, the first fingers of meagre light streaking on the eastern horizon. The flotsam of the wreck has already dispersed, and the sea of corpses has gone. I am truly alone. And then, weaving towards me, I spy a bobbing lantern in the night. I stammer a prayer of thanks to Saint Romain for his mercy.

My saviours are fishermen three, who had heard the cries in the deep, but given the terror and blackness of the night, feared to venture out until first light. Perhaps it was a trick of the wind or waves, but they will tell me later that every cry, every gasp, every prayer was heard on shore by the townspeople of Barfleur. They all had a ringside seat at this tragedy of kings.

Then my fellow Normans haul me down, wrap me in a fresh sheepskin and ferry me safely to their warm harbour. By the time their little boat nears the Cotentin shore, I have slumped into a deep and dreamless sleep.

*   *   *

For weeks, the finely liveried bodies of the Anglo-Norman nobility were washed up on the beaches of Normandy. The catastrophe of the White Ship had claimed some three hundred lives, and Berold, the butcher of Rouen, was the sole survivor. The chronicler Orderic Vitalis recalls that he lived in hale good health for twenty years more, regaling all and sundry with the miraculous tale of his survival. The kingdom of England would not prove so fortunate.

The White Ship proved a harbinger of doom, hanging like a generational curse over England and Normandy alike. The realm was left perilous and naked, without an heir apparent, and in the void, conspiracies would flourish and ambitions fester.

Reports of the shocking tragedy spread fast across the Channel, but even as the nobles reeled in shock at the loss of their sons and brothers, they did not dare break the news to King Henry. His terrible grief and wrath would be too dangerous a beast to rouse.

Eventually the grieving lords stumbled upon an elaborate ruse. They instructed a small and tender boy, barely toddling, to weep before the King. "Why are you crying?", the Sovereign asked. Then the little child stammered out the heart-breaking news: your children are dead. The flower of your nobility perished with them. They say that after that day, King Henry of England never smiled again.

When he died, all hell broke loose. Bitter and protracted wars of succession swept both England and Normandy, plunging both into a cycle of bloody violence. The chroniclers called this time the Anarchy; a time when the royal forest law was broken, when crops turned to seed, and the kingdom withered on the vine.

History had taken a dark and unexpected turn. Soon enough, the entire Angevin empire would founder on the rocks. In 1204, the ancestral homeland of Normandy itself would fall to the French king. Only a scattering of islands would remain, fragments of a lost empire, the wooden flotsam and jetsam from so great a shipwreck.

This is the story of the wreckage left behind from that shipwreck – of Jersey, an island severed from its mother continent a few thousand years before, now shaped and moulded by the sea.

The sea proved its torment and its lifeline, a source of bounty and sorrow. The medieval world was an age of myth and rumour, of fire and darkness. Three early Jersey legends of the sea hold up a mirror to that world. There is doubtless a kernel of truth in each, yet each story was deliberately fashioned to tell a parable; the first to warn of the brutal power of the waves; the second, to avoid the stain of piracy, and the third to expose the folly of overweening greed.

Each one of these stories reveals the desperate need of an island community to maintain social order, to avoid stoking the wrath of foreign powers, and to survive in the treacherous shadow of the sea.

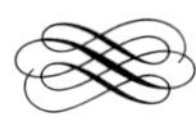

Spring

AGE
OF
LEGENDS

Jersey's Atlantis:
The Lost Manor of La Brecquette

Jersey, September 1356

I will confess this much: I am a trickster, a pilferer, and a thief. I was christened Jean of St Ouen, but I shed that skin on the perquage path, on the day I first slipped away from the Seigneur's justice. That callow youth never returned. In these latter days, I travel under a dozen names, cloaked with a brace of disguises, bound together by a single, burning obsession: for gold.

The moon hung like a gibbet over the western bay on the night I set out to rob the manor of La Brecquette. I was clad in black to hide my face and caked in earth to mask my scent. I darted like a lizard over rocks, skirted the snares of St Ouen's Pond, and followed the stream into the deep valley of l'Etacq. No sound, no voices, no watchmen. The underbelly of my prey lay before me.

The manor house of La Brecquette is old, very old. Some say it is a Roman foreshore fortress, built in the dying days of the Empire. Drunken tongues claim it is practically built on Caesar's buried gold. Yet by my reckoning it looks the same as a dozen other grand Jersey homes; a carcass of heavy red granite, a dower wing and an obligatory tourelle peering balefully over the sandbar towards the western ocean.

The house is surrounded by the finest cider orchards in Jersey. They say the oldest oaks grew on this headland before Helier ever set foot on this blasted rock. Some even say the trees are the last living remnants of an ancient forest, lost to time and memory, dating from the days when the bishop of Coutances could walk over to Jersey on a plank. But I care little for fireside legends. I am here for the coin.

Naturally, if my trespass here were discovered, I would die. I fancy I would be thrown straight off the cliff at Geoffrey's Leap, like felons in days gone by. More likely, I would be hung in the yard of the brutish castle at Mont Orgueil. But the rewards are rich, and the timing is ideal. The Island is distracted, ablaze with joy at the news of the terrific victory at Poitiers. A week of feasting and revelry has been ordained. The wine flows, and the people sleep.

Such quick work to prise a door open, as softly as a feather. The poor guardsmen – farmer lads with pikes – snore like gluttons. I brashly stroll through the dying embers of a lavish feast, through the banqueting chamber. The master of the house, John Wallis, is slumped in his chair, his belly bloated with a surfeit of wine. His hounds are snorting at his feet, chasing rabbits in their dreams. A cloud of maggots in the scullery devours the entrails of a cow, all that is left of the thick joint of gorgeous beef that the master and his guests have enjoyed.

I glide up the spiral stairs like a ghost, and I turn into the strong-room. Yet as I pass the leaden glass window, I stop dead in my tracks. I hear the rushing sound of a mighty river. But there are no great rivers in Jersey. I gasp in dumb amazement, nose pressed against the pane like a child. The sea just beyond the manor is suddenly draining away, beating a sullen, rushing retreat, as if the waters are swirling out of a tub.

They reveal an astonishing world. In the moonlight, I see the broken stumps of a forest, clustered on ledges of rock beyond the sandbar, shelving away from me like terraced steps. So, the old legends were true; there had once been a great wood here, before the age of Noah. His drowned kingdom, of rock palaces and chiselled sea valleys, now stretches away hundreds of yards towards the western horizon.

Fish are floundering on silvery rocks, choking in the fatal air. Eels thrash themselves to death in this strange new world. The black bones of an ancient shipwreck lie exposed on one silted outcrop. Words from my childhood leap unbidden into my mind. 'The first heaven and the first earth had passed away, and there was no longer any sea'.

The red moon glowers in the sky above, as heavy as a stone quern. I glance to the east, where the strong spire of St Ouen's Parish Church still looms against the heights. Yet there is no thunderclap of judgment, no angel-scroll announcing judgment. I cross myself three times, out of instinct. Then I resume my brazen thievery.

My handiwork, as deft as quicksilver, prises open the manorial chest. I scoop my fingers in, and behind a thick ream of title deeds, I finally claim my prize. Silken purses bulging with *livres tournois*, a smattering of rings and jewellery, a fine stash of loot for an evening's work. I fleece the old fool's storehouse in a moment.

Then my head explodes. A brace of seagulls is sweeping in over the tourelle, shrieking in fury. At once the land birds awake in a flurry, whooping together in a cacophony of terror. In the hall below, the wolf-hounds start to howl, as if struck by forked lightning. I freeze. My hand clasps on the hilt of my dagger, my teeth clenched, my heart bursting, ready to fight for my life. Yet the guard-dogs are as giddy as kittens. They thrash straight out of the gates and vanish away into the night, heading up for the higher ground.

A slurred voice yells an oath from the banqueting hall. The master of the house has awoken; the game is up. I sped off into the night, hurtling through the trees as if the hangman himself was at my heels. I ran with every sinew in my body, and I kept on running.

Before long I was panting my innards out, scratched by thorn bushes, my ankle raw and twisted. At last, halfway up the slope of the great hilltop above l'Etacq, I dared to look back.

That was when I saw the great black line on the horizon, unfurling like a scroll, erasing all the stars. A towering ocean wave, the king of tides, was sweeping in at speed towards Jersey. The dreadful wall of black water was five times the height of the tallest man. For an instant, it hung poised, hanging like a curtain over the doomed manor of La Brecquette. Then it fell like an executioner's blade.

A scurry of lanterns; a frantic welter of men saddling up horses, of servants darting like insects in the courtyard. And then that world suddenly drowned, as suddenly and violently as a burning brazier ducked into a pond. The water smashed over the tourelle and all the candles went black. The diabolical wave was not done yet. It ripped on through the rich orchards and surged all the way up the valley of l'Etacq, finally breaking at the foot of the very mount where I cowered. A jagged sea-crest leapt into the sky, salt-spraying my feet, then mercifully folded back onto itself.

I fell to my knees and begged for my life: '*Ave Maria, gratia plena, Dominus tecum…*' Yet just as suddenly as the sea had lurched onto the land, the monstrous tide retreated. It swiftly fell back to its divinely appointed boundaries. Yet the world had changed.

My jaw dropped in awe. The fearsome wave had destroyed the sandbar and punched a new, clean hole in the coast. The map of Jersey had changed in an instant, as if a child had drawn a clean smooth line, an arc right down to Corbière.

And at the low tide next morning, every man could see that the trees and soil of La Brecquette had been stripped away like skin. Only a skeleton of stone remained. Crowds of locals were thronging there, jabbering and pointing, sending salvage boats to bring the debris back home. Already fishermen were scouring for wreck, looting the bricks, swarming like flies on a corpse.

Only this thief had been spared. I wept and prayed for hours. As night fell, I buried my cache of stolen gold, deep beneath the dunes, overlooking the drowned manor. I kept just a single copper coin. I punched a hole in it and will wear it around my neck until the day I die. This will be my albatross, my penance.

*   *   *

And now, of course, it is as if La Brecquette had never been. The years have fallen away like the tide and I am an old man. The endless wars in France still rage of course, like old sores. But the legend of the manor under the sea is a mere fairy tale, a tall story to scare the children on All Hallows' Eve. I still forage for *vraic* on the new foreshore, and tell my tale in the Island's taverns for a sou. The drinkers laugh, and sometimes throw cheap coins to an old fool. At night, I curl and sleep in my rags by the fire-grate, and in my dreams the sky becomes a black wave, and every night those waters are sweeping closer, dragging me home.

I speak not of the gold, buried long ago like the fruit of those drowned orchards. The treasure still lies deep beneath the earth, waiting to be remembered, waiting to be found.

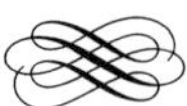

Wreckers of Winter Night

The Chemin de la Brecquette still exists in St Ouen, a road that heads out in a straight line towards the open ocean. At the lowest tides, the stumps of a petrified forest are sometimes revealed. Jersey's myth of a submerged manor house is echoed time and again across the Atlantic world; from the Cornish legend of Lyonesse to the lost city of Ys on Breton shores. The persistence and recurrence of these stories suggests they are more than fireside myths; sober historians remember the great medieval port of Dunwich, indubitably drowned.

The terrifying mutability of the tides was just one aspect of a fearsome cosmos – a world where comets screamed heaven's warnings, where plagues fell without mercy. The abiding image of medieval Europe was the wheel of fortune, that would raise princes to greatness only to turn, and sink them in the mire. Glory was for kings and ambition for fools; the rest must obediently play their part.

A second enduring Jersey story of the sea reveals the folly of mortal ambition, and the retribution that inevitably devours those who shun charity and the law. The 'authorised version' of the legend of the Five Spanish Ships was finally put to paper in the Jersey Tribune *of 1860, but the story is probably centuries old. Listen closely: this is a voice speaking to us from an older, darker world.*

*   *   *

St Ouen's Bay
Late November 1494

Winter had fallen hard upon Jersey. As the red sun collapsed below the western horizon, the sky was smeared with blood. The first breath of frost already sparkled on the higher ground, heralding a bitter night to come. Far to the north, a black storm was brewing.

A gaggle of men was tramping west through the fields, headed for St Ouen's Bay. They were vicious outlaws, bearing halberds, pikes, and skewers – the brutal instruments of war. A motley army, a drunken band of brothers, they wore stolen armour and pilfered boots. Their favourite pastimes were blind drunkenness, spiced with a little light brawling and the occasional murder. The gang of thieves would indulge in every one of these vices in the fearful night to come.

The rolling pastures they strolled through were a byword for bounty. Les Quennevais famously boasted the most fertile fields of the entire Island. Tradition said you merely had to plant an apple seed here in Spring and an orchard would flourish by the autumn.

But these men had neither the patience nor wit for farming. They were predators. When the storms rose, when the waves lashed, they would light beacons on the shore. False fires lured in passing ships, drawing in the weak and the desperate. And when their prey splintered on the rocks at Corbière, they would swoop down like vultures to claim their loot.

And tonight, they had spied five great vessels. They loomed as black as clouds on the sparkling horizon, wounded and limping after some mid-Channel clash, desperate for sanctuary. The galleons seemed frozen on the painted ocean, silhouettes against the dying sun. Tonight, each one of them would be broken on the rocks.

The robbers lit a campfire and threw a bladder of cheap wine around. They were cursing, spitting, mocking the fools who were to be their feast. The old women in the village had, as usual, begged them not to do it. Had not the ground beneath them shaken only the day before, surely a macabre omen? Plundering these ships, they whispered, would only bring ill.

Lamy, a young hothead, scoffed at such cowardly blather. He brandished an arquebus, an exquisite firearm forged by the finest Mediterranean gunsmiths. He had ripped it last winter from the hands of a dying nobleman. His fellow wrecker, Grandin, sharpened his brute hatchet on a rock. As they drank deeper and gorged their imaginations on the plunder ahead, their boasts fell like rain.

Suddenly a stranger stood at the gate of the camp. Who dared to broach this den of thieves? All eyes turned to the intruder, and all hands clasped their weapons. Yet there could be nothing to fear. The visitor was just a frail old man, bent by age, yet pulsing with a wiry strength that belied his years. He wore the faded, tatty robes of a wandering monk. The thieves peered closer at him. There was something strange about his face, something curiously familiar. They could not place it. No matter.

"What do you want, old man?", Grandin sneered.

The stranger fixed them with burning blue eyes, full of sadness and wisdom. He wore a wooden crucifix at his neck, and he spoke with the sorrow of centuries. "Turn back, my friends. Turn back while there is time. The Lord has seen your hearts, and he knows what you are planning. Be warned, my children. If you do not stop now, then His judgment will fall on you, and upon your land".

The robbers howled and hooted with laughter. Then they spat at him and tossed a couple of stones in his direction, shooing him away into the blackness of the night. The wind was whispering by now, then wailing, then shrieking. The storm was coming. Lamy, in a moment of mad exultation, fired his arquebus into the winter night, and the explosion shattered the muggy skies. The gunshot was lost in a volley of thunder, and the first heavy drops of rain began to fall.

The pirates set to work, lighting stacks of brushwood, great flaming bonfires on the headlands, the better to lure the ships to their doom. The galleons, they could see, were soon falling for the ruse. Their masts were broken; like lumbering whales, they would inexorably be dragged in towards the rocks.

Soon enough, the first ship splintered, knifed in the heart by the daggers of Corbière. Place of evil, place of the crows, shunned by all Islanders; but loved by these brigands. They knew well enough the secret passages between the tides, and they swooped in like vultures.

A torrent of broken wood and sailcloth burst upon the shoreline. The ships must have been packed with rich cargo, for barrels and chests floated in the wake of the drowned ship. Lamy and Grandin dashed into the freezing water and grappled to open the first cargo trunk. The clasp on it burst to reveal a trove of silks and jewels.

Then they heard a plaintive cry in the darkness. A small rowing boat, beaten by the waves, had made landfall. It bore three Spanish noblemen, plucked from the sun-drenched palaces of Segovia or Zaragoza, and now hurled upon this wintry rock. And in their midst was a beautiful noblewoman, clutching a tiny, wailing baby.

The pirates paused for a moment, but soon scoffed at the thought of mercy. They made short work of their prey. A crossbow bolt in the heart, the crushing blow of a wrecking-hook: two of the half-drowned noblemen were soon dead. Lamy, in the bloodlust of the attack, let loose his arquebus at the third. A cloud of smoke and acrid powder choked him, and the burst of the shot sent his ears singing. He must have scored a direct hit. Staggering towards him was the bloodied figure who had taken the full force of the blast. Lamy recognised the victim and his heart burst. This man was the spitting image of his own father.

The Lady had broken free from the ambush and had scrambled up a rock. In the moonlight, they could see that she was bedecked in exquisite jewellery, dripping with diamonds and gold, everything the pirates had ever longed for. Her infant child, nestled in her arms, was serene now, strangely beatific despite the howling storm. The wreckers climbed up after her, and soon there were no more ledges left to climb, no routes to safety. The raging sea was around them all, and everywhere, and below.

The Lady turned to face her accusers and cried out to them in a clear and courtly French, their own tongue. "You have preyed on a defenceless woman and her child. This is your reward. Your land will become a desert. No crop will grow there again. And the sea will rise up and claim you all." Then she stepped with her child straight off the rock, down into the abyss of the night.

And as she did so, the earth shook itself like an angry bull shaking off a fly. Lamy and Grandin looked up in terror. The bay itself was turning on the wreckers. A giant funnel-wave, a wall of water as sheer as Gorey Castle, reared up straight ahead of them. The surge was lethal, loaded with ship-timbers and wreckage, primed to shred its victims. The thieves were ripped to ribbons by their own loot. The bodies of the wrecking gang would never be found.

Then, as it made landfall, the waterspout became a great red sandstorm, tearing up into the fertile farms and orchards by the bay. It churned the fields into fine powdery dust, and in its wake came a scorching wall of wildfire. The fields blazed for seven days, burning to the roots. When the ashes were cleared, the rich soil of Les Quennevais had changed. The land had become sand-dunes; a barren waste.

In the deepest days of winter, a frail old man walked there at evening-tide, as the sun sank over the western bay. He placed a wooden cross in the sand and knelt before it, to pray for the souls of the dead.

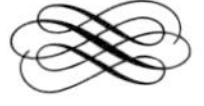

The Legend of the Golden Chair

*T**he hunger for more proves to be the death of men: that was the not-so-hidden message of many a Renaissance tragedy. In an age of the untamed printing press, when popular reformations and revolutions spread like wildfire, human greed was a subversive force. The Governors of Jersey required all of Her Majesty's subjects to stay within the shackles of their ordained rank, to preserve the brittle social order of the realm.*

This morality tale is based on a story first published by William Creed on March 22nd, 1595. It was first published in London, for a metropolitan audience, and despite its specific setting in the bay of Grouville, its Jersey origins are unclear. We do not know if the author, like Shakespeare himself, had simply appropriated an exotic locale for dramatic effect. Alternatively, this may have been a genuine Jersey sea story that found an audience in England's capital, at the zenith of Queen Elizabeth's seafaring age.

Grouville Bay, Jersey
Summer 1594

The wind dropped like a stone. Then the fires of hell burst down over Grouville Bay. Dusk was falling fast, a gathering gloom, and the last fishing boat was hauling in its nets for the night. They were almost empty; it had been a foul catch. The boat masters Dansie and Doughton were barking at their sullen crew, when suddenly their jaws dropped, and they whimpered like puppies.

A dragon's flame was searing across the heavens, a terrifying surge of clean electric blue. The blackened horizon shone brightly for one moment, just like the sun before an eclipse. The sea fizzled with a strong acrid smell of burning. The shipmen fell to their knees in terror. Then the sky collapsed into darkness.

Something was stirring high above the bay. A silent armada was rising over the horizon, but it bore no sails. A flotilla of spheres glowed like lanterns in the sky, with an eerie violet light, pulsing with unearthly energy. They hung there like beautiful, fearsome omens.

Yet all the rest of the world remained still, as if frozen in a dream. Smoke still spilled up from the great grey keep on the heights of Gorey, that mailed fist jutting out towards the Norman coast. The waves continued to lap against the gentle Grouville shore, as gentle as a mother's caress. The beach glistened brightly in the indigo light.

"The fire of Saint Elmo!", whispered the master in awe. Dansie and Doughton were rough men, who spent their days scouring the Duke's seas for fat eels. Dansie was a ruinous peacock of a man, a cocktail of spite and pride. Doughton was a silent, sturdy bully, who spoke best with his fists. The boat's two crewmen, who silently worked the nets like convicts, and sweated every day to make their masters rich, despised them both.

The four fishermen stared at the St Elmo's fire, and then at each other; each one poised somewhere between terror and exultation, fear and astonishment. Then Dansie's twisted face broke into a rare smile, revealing a brace of rotten teeth, some repaired with soft gold. He declared: "This is a sign of good fortune, boys. Head for the old wreck at once – and haul the nets in afresh."

At those words, the ghost-lights fled. Then the winds rose, and a storm crashed in, and firecrackers of lightning whipped over the water. The waves were high, and the fishing boat lurched in the storm. Yet the crewmen, drenched and seething with resentment, sailed out one last time, and cast the net.

The nets had torn. The first one was ripped open like a goose at Yuletide. The men eventually hauled the second net in, sweating like oxen, but a great deadweight was holding them back. Their muscles bulged at the exertion, but at last they landed their cargo on the shore. Dansie sauntered over to survey his prize.

At first, draped with tentacles of sea-weed, the nature of this wreck was hard to decipher. Yet even in twilight, and beneath a crust of rust, this catch glimmered. It was a heavy object, of weighty metal. Dansie's heart clammed up in his chest and the blood drained from his face. This was made of clean, beaten gold. It was the throne of a fallen king.

The men gasped. They had all heard tell of Plato's Atlantis, and seen the tree-stumps at low tides that ringed the coasts of Jersey. Great kings must have ruled here once, giant men in ancient forests before the Flood drowned the world. Before them lay the astonishing proof.

A miracle had been dragged ashore. Upon closer inspection, the golden throne was carved in the form of a tree, with a hundred intertwined branches rising from the heart-root of the royal bloodline. Yet further up the seat, the leaves became thorns, and the branches had holes and embossed seals, ending in spikes and razor-ridges. Was this an instrument of power or torture, or perhaps both? What beauty had this throne witnessed, and what cruelty?

It mattered not. This treasure could buy a castle; a brace of manor houses; a whole Island. So Dansie and Doughton stepped aside to confer, as thick as thieves. Dansie, a flicker of fear rippling across his soft neck, urged caution: "Let us sell this treasure and give the men a hundred pounds apiece. They know our secret; let us buy their silence". Yet Doughton was unyielding as a boulder: "These men deserve nothing. Given them a week's wages and send the fools home to drink it away."

The boat-men were muttering too, wielding darker oaths and angrier words: "These greedy churls should not deprive us of the treasure. We hauled in the net; we dragged up this treasure. These leeches shall have none of it."

And without a word, the first meaty crewman grabbed his boathook, a long pike of wood, with a vicious spike at its tip, and plunged it towards his hated masters. Dansie was struck by surprise, and collapsed with barely a whimper, like a broken marionette. Doughton blurted out an oath, but the sheer force of the impact sent him spinning to the ground. Their blood stains mingled deep into the sand, and the rising tide swept their bodies from sight. The golden chair glimmered with pride in the clear moonlight.

Panic leapt in. Murder had been committed; the Bailiff would soon enough string them up like lambs. Where could the guilty crewmen run? They had to head for France.

So, they lugged the heavy throne into the skiff and headed out to the rocks. Yet the going was hard. Somewhere beyond the Ecréhous, a gang of unknown sailors in an unmarked pinnace came alongside. They offered help; a little too effusively, for they had spied the astonishing treasure and sought to claim it as their own. Out in the turbulent sea, daggers were drawn with these strange assailants, and a brief and bloody skirmish erupted. As they veered off away into the night, one of the two Jersey sailors lay dying.

The last surviving fisherman panicked; he could not sail this boat alone. The French shore was looming up fast, so he wrapped the golden chair in a sail and leapt out with it into the choppy brine. It was a madcap gamble. He could not hold his treasure; the weight was too great. The cursed chair slipped back into the waves, plunging back down to the drowned kingdom of the forest.

The next morning, the fisherman was found washed up on the Norman shore, somewhere near Granville. They tried to save him of course, but he was already cut too deep, his limbs pulverised by the reefs. He was utterly delirious, babbling some tale of a golden throne, of a terrible treasure lost under the waves.

At the third watch of night he died, and they buried him by the foreshore, in the stranger's cemetery. No-one ever learned his name.

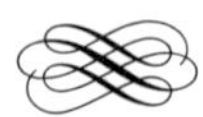

Summer

AGE
OF
ADVENTURE

To the Promised Land:
De Carteret's Settling of Sark

As the old stories confirmed, the sea was Jersey's cloak; its shield, and also its gaoler. It had always been so. And then the old world began to change. We step from the world of legends to the dawn of the scientific age. The old order of popes and kings, of maps with known and familiar boundaries, began to change.

The world was becoming new. The astonishing horizons of the Americas opened up, and Jersey fishermen were among the very first to plunder the Grand Banks of Newfoundland and exploit the riches of strange new lands.

Sir Walter Raleigh, soon to be an ambitious Governor of Jersey, was plotting fresh colonies on the coast of Virginia, the land named after his Queen. The Americas, of course, carried only the illusion of wilderness, for the land was already brimming with rich and ancient cultures.

Yet strangely, in this same age, one of Jersey's closest neighbours had genuinely fallen into emptiness and ruin. For the Island of Sark had become a place unpeopled and untamed. Rabbits over-ran abandoned fields, and brambles slowly strangled ancient ruins. This is the story of the bold plan to reclaim Jersey's forgotten sister isle, and to establish a new colony there, on the edge of the ocean.

Helier de Carteret
Jersey, 1564

I have lived my whole life brooding in its shadow. As a child, I would gaze out to sea, from my family's ancestral lands of St Ouen. I would stand high up in the tower at Grosnez, where the cliffs collapse like grey ash into the sea. The old castle keep is falling to ruin, but a brazier still burns day and night to warn off foreign ships.

Looking north, Sark dominated the far horizon, like a promise or a warning. Behind its sheer, inaccessible cliffs, it always seemed fertile and green enough. Yet that great wilderness was empty of human souls. No feet walked on that high plateau any longer; no forges burned, and no mills turned. The land had gone to seed; they said fields had swallowed up the roadways, and the monastery had fallen betwixt thorns and brambles.

Like the moon shining in the winter sky, Sark lay empty and bright, so tantalisingly close that a man might simply stretch out his arm and reach it. Yet it was cleaved from us by a fierce channel, bristling with a fringe of razor reefs. Who would cross that great gulf between us?

We grew up on the legends of Saint Magloire, who slew a red dragon in Jersey, and then struck north to build a monastery in Sark. We heard tell of the golden days of the past, when Sark nestled under the wing of the Warden of the Isles, and a pretty water-mill ground corn for bread. Then the four horsemen of the apocalypse fell upon us; endless wars, the terror of plague, the failed harvests at summer's end, and the harrowing of the French raiders.

When the Black Death ravaged these Isles, and the winters turned fierce and full of ice, Sark was abandoned. It remained a sentinel on the northern horizon, a watchman at sunset. Like the mysterious stone circles that guard our parish, I had a strange sense that it was watching and waiting for us.

Kings and queens fell, and the wheel of fortune turned. Religious passions swept the world, and my uncle, the Bailiff of Jersey, was one of the foremost advocates of the reformed faith. He only wished, he often told me, to strip away the accretions of the centuries and return to the pure simplicity of the original faith. He was determined, he said, to return *ad fontem* – to the source.

And I too wished to make my way back to a place that had been forgotten. Sark loomed in the night, a shadow under a carpet of stars, abandoned to the rabbits and rainstorms. It glowered at us from across the sea-channel, a herald of our frailty, a witness to our decline. Onfrey de Carteret had sailed to victory with the Conqueror, and my ancestors had been lords of St Ouen since time immemorial. We rightfully claimed to be the premier fief in Jersey, yet we lay vulnerable to attack from the north, should any passing marauder happen to seize that realm.

I felt a burning, fierce determination that I would be the man to restore the fortunes of my house and my Island. I would strike north and reclaim that which had been lost for too long. It was time for Sark to return to the world of men.

*   *   *

They say this is an age of discovery – wilderness everywhere is being tamed, and the vastness of the New World is opening up its riches. Beyond the Pillars of Hercules, men have found and plundered cities of gold. New territories are falling like fruit into the courts of Europe. The time for my project is ripe.

Closer to home, the French have been harrying at our heels, as wars of religion tear Europe apart and England embroils itself in the fray. Rouen fell in the bitter siege of 1562; the threat is nearing our shores. Invasion is our secret dread, lurking at the pit of every stomach, and we are in Jersey are fearfully exposed to the north. Five years ago, the Seigneur of Glatigny tried to establish an encampment on Sark;

the outbreak of hostilities scared him off, but the scope of French ambition is clear.

So, I made my bold proposal to the Crown. I dared to claim the fief of Sark, saying I would gladly shoulder the burden alongside the boon. I would bind myself by oath to establish a permanent settlement on the Island, and to defend it at my own cost. The Captain of Guernsey, who had nominal responsibility yet little stomach for its defence, was happy to oblige. At a stroke, I had taken a thorny and perplexing problem from his grasp and made it my very own. As a final sweetener, I also agreed to pay fifty *sols tournois* every year into the Crown Receiver of Guernsey's velvet-lined pockets.

We made first landfall in the summer of 1564. Our boat set off north, past the three vicious rocks of the Pierre de Lecq upon which so many ships have foundered. We pushed up through strong tidal channels, until we drifted in the shadow of those great Sark cliffs, that tower some three hundred and sixty feet above the churning sea. Sark, we were reminded, is a curious creature; its southernmost head hangs only by the thinnest of necks, like a swan, to the main body of the Island. Mark my words: crawling on that hog's back to Little Sark in high winds, threatened by a sheer fall to oblivion on either side, you will soon discover the true force of a storm.

As we steered our craft north, we noted that Sark has no harbours, no natural coves or landing places. Unlike a Bouley or a Grève de Lecq, even where a little beach may be found, there is no easy path to the interior. After scouting the shore, sculling through a moonscape of rocks and gleaming caves, we eventually beached at the foot of the cliffs they call l'Eperquerie. In distant, happier times, when men dwelt here, fishermen would haul in eels and hang them on poles on the fields far above, to cure in the sun. Generations of conger hunters had cut a precarious path down to the shore, and the trail still remained, so we followed it up to the heights.

That summer we cleared just enough brambles in Sark to cut a field, and we planted a simple square of crops, nothing more. We put the soil to the test, and the wheat flourished remarkably. As the chroniclers had predicted, this was rich and fertile ground. We brought the first bushels of Sarkese corn home for milling.

Next Spring, we promise ourselves, we shall sail north again, and this time there will be no return journey. This time we must settle in this strange wilderness, a place in its own way as curious and wild as the Americas and make it our own. In the year of our Lord 1565, I will leave behind the sumptuous halls of St Ouen's Manor. Next year, when we land our boats again before the cliffs of l'Eperquerie, we will be coming home.

*　　*　　*

Whitehall Palace
London, 1572

Queen Elizabeth's hair is burning flame; her face glistens as white as marble. She sits in immaculate repose, bedecked with amber jewels, and her pale cheeks and neck are smothered with the finest Venetian ceruse. Her ladies-in-waiting are clad in black; mere fading stars before the blinding orbit of their radiant Sun. I dare not look directly into the Queen's dark brown eyes, encircled with black kohl, but I can already feel them dissecting me, prising me open. She sits here on the throne of kingdoms, as terrifying as her father Henry before her. No wonder the very princes of Europe are putty in her hands, as they jostle to court her favour.

After our ship docked at Greenwich, we fought through the maelstrom of London to reach her, through the squalor and glory of her capital. Perhaps it is the overwhelming sprawl of the City, or the sublime power of royal blood, or the simple gravity of my petition, but I stand before her dumbstruck.

Here my name and title carry little weight; the meanest nobles at her court boast hunting grounds that would easily swallow up the whole of St Ouen. I am a mere stranger, unversed in courtly finery, summoned to behold her beauty from the outer orbit of her galaxy. What might Jersey itself mean to her – is it just another beautiful ornament, a rock on her neck? Of what possible importance is Sark, which would barely squeeze into one of her royal parks?

And yet the Queen seems most interested in my curious tale, the story of how we have planted England's newest and closest colony. For in the April of 1565, my wife and I landed again on Sark, and this time we made it our home. This land yielded us nothing at first: no tracks, no shelter and no trees. We found only ruins; the fallen arches of a monastery, the blackened shell of the oratory where Magloire himself must have prayed a thousand years past.

It has been relentless, arduous work; clearing the thick brambles, building shelter amidst the ruins, planting the harvest. But the eventual prize will be worth it. Some believe there may be buried treasure here; others whisper that the rocks of the Isle may even bear silver. I know not the truth of these rumours, but I have been glad to let these impressions stand.

That summer, Queen Elizabeth awarded me Letters Patent that secured my right to the Island, 'void, waste and uninhabited' as it was. Should I fail to inhabit the Island, the fines would be punitive, and I would forfeit my rights. Yet I succeeded in my task, and the settlement is a success. So, this year, she is going to elevate Sark to the status of a 'Fief Haubert' in its own right, independent of my ancestral seat of St Ouen, to be awarded to my heirs in perpetuity. I am to become the first Lord of Sark.

In honour of the occasion, I have presented my Queen with a map of Sark embossed with gold, as lavish an artwork as I can afford. My cartographers have mapped the Isle and beautifully illuminated every contour of Her Majesty's new realm. Each pleasing cove and bay has been adorned with ornamental filigree, shimmering as magically as any realm of the Indies.

Her Majesty seems very pleased. To tame a virgin island, to settle in a wilderness, and above all, to keep it out of French hands, is a feat she is only too happy to acknowledge. She holds out a charter for me, and as I see the herald unfurl it, I kneel before her again to offer my solemn homage to the Crown, to accept the 'Fief Haubert' of Sark. Her piercing dark brown eyes fix me like a butterfly pinned to a board. For the moment, my hopes hang by a thread, as slender as the neck of La Coupée. Then she utters the words: "I accept you as my man and Lord of Sark".

My heart is bursting with joy. And I can see that Elizabeth, by the Grace of God, of England, France and Ireland, Queen, Defender of the Faith, and my beloved Duke of Normandy, is smiling.

*   *   *

The wilderness of Sark took decades to tame. As if Helier de Carteret was sculpting a strange new world, the landscape of the island needed to be utterly transformed. First the brambles were burned, the warrens cleared, and the open fields enclosed. The skin of Sark was carved up like meat, into forty fresh parcels of land, awarded to forty loyal tenants. Thirty-five of the tenants were Jersey families, and the remainder hailed from Guernsey. De Carteret chose the choicest and most central location, Le Manoir by the Dixcart Valley, for himself. The isle was swiftly cultivated; orchards were planted, and oxen and horses brought to the land. The ruined watermill at l'Ecluse began to grind fresh wheat. The arms of a windmill turned on the highest point of the island.

Then the colonists laboured to build roads, wide and straight, much broader than the meandering lanes of Jersey and more akin to the fledgling thoroughfares of a New World city. Hedges were planted to seal the land, to mark property and ownership. Grand houses were built at the heads of streams.

As Nature had so dismally failed to provide a convenient harbour, the ingenuity of Renaissance engineering would have to provide one instead. There was indeed a perfect landing place, but it was severed from the interior by a wall of rock. So, De Carteret simply used gunpowder to blast a massive hole in the rock that men could pass straight through. The gaping entrance became known as 'Le Creux', or 'the Hole'; and his tenants constructed a stone breakwater there.

Queen Elizabeth was delighted with her glittering map. In return she provided a gift for Helier de Carteret, first Lord of Sark; a freshly forged set of field guns to defend his new domain. She had the barrel of one inscribed to mark the occasion: Don de sa Majesté La Royne Elizabeth au Seigneur de Sark AD 1572.

The gilded map is lost forever. The cannon remained. They guarded the Seigneurie, watching and waiting for the invaders who never came, until they did at last, bearing the banner of an eagle and a twisted cross, in an age beyond all imagining.

* * *

De Carteret had secured Sark for the Crown, and the northern flank of Jersey was no longer easy meat for any passing fleet. Yet in an age of imperial rivalry and confessional war, effective maritime defences remained of paramount importance. The military engineer Paul Ivy designed a new castle for Jersey in St Aubin's Bay, and its construction began.

In 1600, Queen Elizabeth sent a flawed jewel of the age to oversee progress; a man who encapsulated all its cruelty and brilliance, its folly and its contradictions. Sir Walter Raleigh, the new Governor of Jersey, was the quintessential Elizabethan adventurer, a poet who carefully cultivated his own legend as assiduously as his harvest of Virginia tobacco. He was sage and seafarer, entrepreneur and pirate, a nobleman at court and a butcher on the battlefield.

Raleigh proved no absentee Governor of Jersey, rather a whirlwind of energy and enthusiasm who personally ruled his domain. He established a land registry, resolved bitter local quarrels with the wisdom of a Solomon, and saved Gorey Castle itself from demolition. He urged on the building of the new fortress and dedicated it in honour of his beloved Queen: Fort Isabella Bellissima; *Elizabeth the most beautiful. Today it remains one of Jersey's cherished landmarks.*

Yet his present was already becoming our past, slipping away into history. When his Queen died in 1603, and King James of Scotland moved south to claim the throne, Raleigh's fortunes turned. He was charged with treason, convicted and locked in the Bloody Tower in London.

Imprisoned in his study, his mind was free to range over the wide terrains of alchemy and art, science and scholarship. He penned a literary masterpiece, a million words sweeping over the history of humanity. The walls of the Tower had become his world; the high seas a memory; Jersey a strange dream. And then one night, after nearly thirteen long years, a key turned in the door.

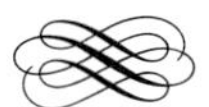

Under the Line: Raleigh's Last Voyage

'I have a long journey to go, and therefore will take my leave'.
(Sir Walter Raleigh, on the scaffold, 1618)

At last the walls parted and the Tower spat me out. After so many years of incarceration, I was myself a carcass, shuffling along on my dead leg, an old man rasping his way through an unfamiliar world. Here I was: Sir Walter Raleigh; poet, adventurer and mage, adrift on strange new seas.

London has changed in these latter times, and the hearts of men have turned. The city of my youth, that once dazzled with all the colours of a Guiana parrot, has turned dark and sombre. Men wear plainer, duller clothes; the panache of Queen Elizabeth's reign has fled. The fabric of the city itself has darkened, with new halls and monuments. London is forever restless, forever becoming something new. I ride through the familiar streets as if in a dream.

Queen Elizabeth, the lodestar of my life, now lies frozen in marble. Her effigy is entombed in her father's royal chapel at Westminster Abbey. I stopped and gazed awhile at her, at that face serene as the moon, as cold as the winter skies. My fate was sealed at the very moment the last breath fled her body. The new King James soon turned on me like a wolf.

I fondly remember my final days before the fall, when I held the Queen's stewardship of a most beautiful realm. I was the Governor of Jersey, my last haven before the prison walls closed in on me. From my perch at Mount Orgueil, I reigned as a happy little monarch, dispensing justice, establishing a land registry, and overseeing construction of a new fortress in the bay. Some urged that brute old Mount Pride should now be demolished, but I demurred. I captured my thoughts in a letter: '*To say true, it is a stately fort of great capacity… And if a small matter may defend it, it were a pity to cast it down*'. As it happened, I would be the great and ancient castle that would fall.

In those painful years in the Tower, I never forgot my beloved Island. In my long decade of captivity, I poured my sorrows into my *History of the World*, my vainglorious and voluminous manuscript, which they have forced me to publish as an anonymous man. Jersey was too painful to my heart, too close a device to reveal; but I revelled in recounting the valiant history of neighbouring Sark.

In the dog watch of the evening, the gaoler's key turned in the door. I was at last released; free in some manner of speaking, yet not at liberty, never absolved. An armed watchman escorted me at all times. And I have been sent out for one purpose only: to discover new worlds for the King, and to bring peaceably home a ship laden with gold. And if I openly clash with the Spaniards, or resort to piracy, the King will claim my head.

Remember this: I am legally dead. I have already been tried and convicted by the courts of England, and my execution remains a legal certainty. It is only the timing and manner that is open to review. Nothing has changed.

And yet my fresh letters patent from the King have given me martial command of a fleet, and the power to enforce life and death is once again placed in my hands. Yet the wily old fox has altered the traditional form of the document; the words 'trusty and well beloved' have been deliberately struck out. I know I am walking as if on a wire, high above a void, with all the world waiting for me to fall.

I am grown poor in my dotage; my release was secured not by my heartfelt pleas but by several plump and astutely placed bribes. I have poured my own plate and mortgaged my treasure into this last expedition, this final throw of the dice. I have assembled a surly crew of misbegotten rogues and thieves. They have already squabbled with the Plymouth locals and come up worse the wear in a riverine fight. Their discipline is appalling, and if truth be told, even my beloved son Wat is a brawling hothead. It will be a miracle if we leave port in good order, let alone complete our madcap mission.

We will be travelling far south, towards the burning equatorial sun, to find the City of Gold. Long ago, on my travels in Guiana, a trader brought me some shards of rock, flecked with gold ore. The natives spoke in reverent tones of a great table-mountain, where the cliffs shimmer with rainbows of gold, and the hills bleed silver. Somewhere beyond must lie Lake Parime, and the shining city of El Dorado itself. I let that enticing vision sustain me in my cell and drive me half-mad with its promise. In the end, I almost believed in it. In the fevers of the night I can see the way there: it is always three miles hence, always further beyond, just another turn in the river.

Now I face a stark choice: to find this gold or die. I am in the autumn of my years now. My leg pains me daily, for I am betrayed by the splinters of an old wound. Still the crowds flock to me; this relic, a curio, a grey-haired myth that somehow lingers on from Elizabeth's glorious age. As we march down to the quayside, the good burghers of Plymouth cheer and beat the drums in unison. The West still remembers, even as the capital forgets their fallen hero, and treats me like just another man they used to know.

I board my flagship, as we prepare to set off round the Plymouth Hoe, to leave England for the last time. My ship bears a proud, almost theatrical name: *Destiny*.

Life is but a play, after all. The audience are cheering and hooting from the galleries as I strut into the third act of my life. I bow low and walk up the gangplank, back onto the stage. Somewhere beyond, I can sense the shadow of the axe waiting in the wings.

Guiana
Mouth of the Orinoco
Saint Valentine's Day, 1618

The weather waxed foul, and within hours of leaving, we scurried like rats back to Plymouth. It was a humiliating volte-face. The onward voyage proved no more enabling. Battered by fresh gales at the Scillies, hemmed in at Cork for three miserable and rain-sodden weeks, we had already lost the meat of the summer. Eventually, as tempers flared and mutiny brewed, the weather spun in our favour and our little expedition broke south at last.

I was resolved at first to keep a godly ship. Psalters and divine service; clean mouths and penitent hearts; all an utter charade. The men were wild dogs, driven reckless by fleas of grievance and mutinous at the first pangs of discomfort. The sea was broiling; as our barrels dwindled and our thirst grew, the Canaries at last beckoned. We were bold to land on Spanish soil, when ambassador Gondomar's letters had doubtless poisoned the wells ahead of us, but we had little choice. So, we anchored before the bleak volcanic craters of Lanzarote, and we bartered for bread. We came in peace, we said, and we solemnly pledged to stay close to shore.

My men disobeyed me. Three of them went in deep and alone, swaggering into the heart of the Island. They brawled, and daggers were drawn, and only one staggered back alive. We had proved ourselves scoundrels. At sunset, we fled onwards, to the arid harbour of Gran Canaria, to treat with the Lieutenant of the Canaries himself. In the drought of summer, there was little succour. In green Gomera, we found fresh clean water, and newly emboldened, we set off again, skirting the coast of Africa, buffeted by storms, our supplies dwindling.

West of the Cape Verde Islands, we were suddenly becalmed. The ocean was now a polished mirror, with the image of our phantom ship printed upon it. The sun became a fireball. Swarms of weevils burst into our pantry, devouring the ship's biscuits in a feeding frenzy. Then the winnowing of the heat started to crack open the boards, steam our bodies, and inflame our minds. We saw that shining city of Guianese gold in every blazing, infernal sunset.

In the fever of the night, we slept on the open deck. Magellan's Cloud was our heavenly comforter –a wispy dandelion's head of stars, high in the blazing sky. It seemed as unsullied as a pluck of white Jersey wool. As every astronomer will know,

Magellan's Cloud is the hallmark of the southern hemisphere. As a simple matter of mathematics, the astrolabe told us we must be clinging on above, somewhere a few degrees above the great divide. In our minds, it was too late: we had already slipped under the line.

And then the deaths began. The ocean was a broiling soup-bowl, and the ship stank. Stark calm, extreme hot; we were scourged in this purgatory without hope of release. Death stalked the ship. One by one, my friends succumbed: Fowler, Moore, Crab, Talbot; all men loyal and true, and I would never see their like again.

Then I slipped myself on the burning stairway, on my Jacob's Ladder, and my old wound erupted in flames. A fever consumed me. For twenty days I thrashed like an eel on my bed, sweating and hallucinating. I changed my flamboyant, silken shirts thrice daily and thrice nightly, and still they were sodding and stinking. Their peacock finery mocked my agony.

I lay confined abed like a woman in labour, unable to sleep, buffeted by agonies. I dreamed oftentimes of the gentle slopes of Jersey, of the comely orchards and the magnificent bay, the soothing autumn rains, the cool valleys of St Peter and its gentle brooks and mills. I fondly remembered the amusement I provided by striking up my pipe, when wreathed in smoke like a warlock, I addressed the truculent States of Jersey. Happy days; forever lost.

I gulped water like a fish, even as the last casks from the Canaries ran dry, and barely a stewed prune passed my lips for a month. I am a sailor, and have faced many terrible hardships, but none proved so dread as this pestilence. It felt as if a robber had smashed me over the head with a rock on the road to Jericho and left me to die. That rock, I have lately come to see, was my own pride. 'And if a small matter may defend it, it were a pity to cast it down...'

The heat permeated the ship, infiltrating my bones. It felt like time itself burning up. We painstakingly crawled across the fiery ocean, until we finally arrived on the shores of the world beyond.

On the eleventh day of November, the smudge of a continent stained the horizon. This at last is Guiana, the fabled land we remembered from years past, the rainforest straddling the Equator. Somewhere in its dark heart, deep betwixt the rivers Amazon and Orinoco, lies El Dorado, the fabled city of gold.

We anchored somewhere on the edge of the immeasurable forest, perched on the fringes of this green and impassable ocean. Here we gorged ourselves at last on berries and Casavi bread, roasted mullets, plantains and pistachios; the fruit of the kingdom. A little armadillo meat gradually restored my spirits. We had been grievously afflicted; yet at the last, we had survived.

The Caroni is a blackwater river, red and sluggish, charged with the blood of the land. Somewhere along it lies Mont Aio, which I had once seen with my own eyes: a great and high plateau, many miles across, raised stark above the forest like Jersey above the sea. And deep in the wilderness beyond must lie the magic mountain; whose very pebbles are nuggets of gold ore, whose very cliffs are stained with silver. This mother lode will be enough.

Yet I was too weak to follow on. My best and most loyal friends were dead. So, I chose what poor cards I could from my frail hand: I selected Lawrence Keymis, seadog and rogue, doubter and ditherer. He would lead the expedition west to the heart of the Orinoco, to search and find the gold. The success of our mission rested on his shoulders. Into his protection I placed my beloved Walter, my eldest son, the very image of me. Hot-headed and strong, blood of my blood, fault of my stars.

Then their pinnace, their little band of adventurers, sailed out to meet the sunset. As darkness fell over my ship, I little guessed in my heart that the mission had already failed. The ink had spilled on my death warrant. The axe had already dropped.

Two days later, we witnessed the marvel of a double rainbow, a perfect circle breaking behind the ship. For a moment, I briefly recalled the divine promise: 'And it shall come to pass, when I bring a cloud over the earth, that the bow shall be seen in the cloud: and I will remember my covenant'. Then the bow faded, and I returned to my obsessive quest for gold.

There was no news from Keymis. We loitered in the swamp-lands of the Orinoco, at the Serpent's Mouth itself. Here a native guide led us into the rainforest, to show us the balsam tree, sticky and sweet-smelling. The balm of Gilead, the men called it. The name sits aright. The days dripped on.

There was no news from Keymis. I counted each day since the expedition departed; and I anxiously toyed with the hourglass in my cabin. I mused on the strange alchemy of time, and its promise of transmutation, which changes the elements of all things, and leaves nothing undone. Child into man, earth into gold, fame into dust. I thought of the walls of my prison, of all those years consumed. The nature of time must be heat after all; rising, infiltrating, burning. We ate sweet blood oranges in the sunset, the flesh as bright as the dying sun.

The next morning, a letter was thrust into my hand. The sun died. The hourglass emptied.

*   *   *

The expedition, as the letter revealed, had slipped into bloody, tragic disaster. Keymis had expected to find a few huts in the jungle, and gold mines lying wide open to plunder. Yet the world had changed since the glory days of their earlier expedition some twenty-three years earlier. Instead, the motley band of adventurers stumbled upon San Thomé; a walled and fortified Spanish town. Inevitably, the blunderers were discovered, and a full-scale gunfight ensued. They say that Raleigh's son, Wat, stood at the head of the charge, recklessly storming the gates of the citadel. He was cut down like a stray dog.

The city fell; but there was no gold, and the wrath of the Spanish Empire would soon be falling upon them. King James could not forgive this flagrant breach of international relations. In despair, the little expedition scouted hundreds of miles upriver, scouring every cove and bend of the Orinoco for treasure; they found nothing. Talk of the golden city was on every tongue, the common currency of the rainforest, but it remained a stubborn, elusive mirage.

On his return to the ship, Lawrence Keymis found his master Sir Walter shredded by grief, in a vengeful and unforgiving temper. Keymis knew his duty; after a few days, he retreated to his cabin and shot himself in the chest with a pistol. When the gunshot agonisingly misfired in his ribs, he slashed open his own heart.

His sacrifice was to no avail. Raleigh wrote in a letter: 'My brains are broken'. The suicide of Keymis barely registered; he was lost in the abyss of his own pain. Men deserted; the expedition was crumbling around him like fool's gold. The crew refused to return to the Orinoco. On the journey home, Raleigh could have slipped away in Trinidad, or Newfoundland, or France, or chosen one of a dozen opportunities to escape, but he refused. The show must go on and the play enter its final and most terrible act.

The rest of the script is well-known. The voyage of the Destiny *had been cursed; it proved the shipwreck of all their estates. Gondomar, the silver-tongued Spanish ambassador, soon twisted King James's mind against this rogue adventurer who had betrayed him. Over bowls of plump cherries, they plotted revenge together.*

Visionary, alchemist and scholar, Raleigh had been the finest Governor of Jersey, yet was ultimately broken on the wheel of his own pride. On the scaffold, he dazzled the crowds for one last time, defending his life and his record with wit, passion and eloquence. He scoffed at the axe: "This is a sharp medicine, but it is a physician that will cure all my diseases". Then he placed his head on the block.

Raleigh refused a blindfold. Chided at the very last for kneeling away from the east, away from the Lord's rising, he replied with one final rejoinder: "So the heart be right, it is no great matter which way the head lieth". Yet his heart was already lost somewhere on a faraway shore.

Then a strange and curious silence fell upon the crowd, and the last moment seemed to stretch for an eternity. As Raleigh the poet had once written, 'Even such is time that takes in trust / Our youth, our joys, our all we have / And pays us but with age and dust ...'

Raleigh's severed neck spurted so much blood that the spectators gasped. Such energy, such promise, so many worlds left undiscovered. The crowd lamented and sighed and shuffled back to work. Above them, it was threatening to rain. A pall of smoke rose awhile over the palace yard, languidly turning, then vanished up into the autumn skies.

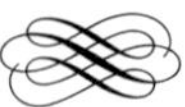

Charles Robin: The Fisher King

The restless spirit of the age did not die with Raleigh. The simmering tensions between a headstrong people and overmighty kings would eventually erupt into civil war, and Jersey played a prominent part in that story. George de Carteret, the Bailiff of Jersey, was loyal to the last. In Jersey, he would offer shelter to the fugitive young King Charles and his little brother the duke of York in their darkest hour.

Jersey shrugged off the fire and chaos of the war years, and the long interlude of the Commonwealth, to emerge at the heart of the seafaring Atlantic world. De Carteret's dogged loyalty to the Crown in its years of adversity yielded rich rewards. He was granted a share in a vast tract of land in the Carolinas. James, Duke of York, fresh from lending his name to a promising American seaport, decided to cede him another prime portion of Atlantic coastline. This new land was rich and fair, and de Carteret would name it after the Island of his birth. He called it 'New Jersey'.

The Island of Jersey would yield its own crop of adventurers. Another de Carteret, Philippe, son of the Seigneur of Trinity, would circumnavigate the world. In 1767, as captain of HMS Swallow, he stumbled upon Pitcairn Island, an uninhabited volcanic outcrop in the Pacific Ocean. The new Island was named after the midshipman on his watch who had spotted it.

Meanwhile, Jersey's economic might waxed stronger than ever in the seas of the Atlantic; above all in Newfoundland and the wilder reaches of the Gaspé peninsula. The Island's monopoly on its cod fisheries would be the bedrock of its prosperity for centuries. It was largely the work of one man, a single-minded titan of industry, one of Jersey's founding fathers. He was a lean, wily and ambitious trader from St Aubin called Charles Robin. This is his story.

*   *   *

Paspébiac, Chaleur Bay
Province of Lower Canada
February 1802

A fireship is burning in the bay. It is the night before the storm, in the darkest hours, and a plume of snow is brewing over the sea, poised to strike. I can feel the air is charged, the skies primed and loaded like the barrel of a gun.

I was born in gentle St Aubin, but that life ended thousands of miles away across the ocean. It lingers only as memory, a waning fragment of something half-forgotten. Here in my winter quarters at Paspébiac, on the western shores of the North Atlantic, I dwell alone. I awoke this morning at an unearthly hour, as the chill burrowed deep into my bones, my back and legs aching now as the accumulated years extract their brutal toll. I am too old to relent now, too old to let go.

So as my fellow shareholders nestle by their Jersey firesides or in their London salons, I am still buried alive here in the snow, an ageing troglodyte, holed up in these wooden caves. Some mornings, even my daily bread takes an hour to thaw. It is too late to sleep, too soon to rise. So, I stumble, drunken with exhaustion, up to the terrace that faces the sea. The window is framed with fresh icicles, like the crown of a winter king.

The world outside gleams a blinding, virgin white. The sea is simmering under the burning disc of the full moon. I gaze towards the staggering mountains of the interior, their waterfalls frozen in mid-flow. The trees that flank them are carpeted in thick snow. My gaggle of wooden fishery buildings cling closer to the shore, where the encroaching snowdrifts threaten to choke the thin beach and reach right to the water's edge.

I am rasping in the chilly night, each lungful as vital and shocking as the first breath of a baby. I peer into the winter night. And that's when first I see it, a ship coming in from the east, sweeping in from the horizon.

The ship is on fire. Three pillars of burning flame, a mast ablaze. It is magnificent, this ship of the dead. I have seen this herald before. I know it always comes right before the storm. Some say the ghost ship is an apparition, a curse, left over from the earliest centuries of exploration and plunder; Iberian pirates damned to burn by the very natives they sought to enslave. It blazes before me like a torch warning of the Armada, or perhaps the Viking funeral ships that men say once burned on these shores. For a brief moment, it hangs on the horizon, breathing fire.

The ice is seeping into my blood. My limbs are rattling with the sheer cold, twitching involuntarily like a marionette. But I am bewitched by the ghostly flames. Then a black cloudbank explodes in the sky, and the fireship is smothered out. Within minutes, the snowstorm swoops down.

As I retreat back to the meagre warmth of my bedchamber, my mind is ranging far across that vast and turbulent ocean. I am busy calculating a dozen profit margins in my mind, judging the price that a thousand quintals of dried cod will fetch in Madeira next Spring.

I am forever juggling a hundred calculations; a score of fears and a dozen schemes. My philosophy has always been to build my empire steadily, cautious and slow, hoarding every farthing. As sleep claims me again, I am basking somewhere in the warm sunshine of Santander, watching as my cod-ships roll in and the quays fill up with rich goods for the return leg of my trade.

I have sweated blood to build my maritime kingdom. I was twenty-three years old when I left the Island of Jersey and first set sail for the New World. We landed amongst the *barachois*, the curious sandbars that wrinkle the coast hereabouts, framing pretty little lagoons. As soon as we landed, I started to trade with the local settlers. I negotiated relentlessly through the night, bartering, bargaining, biting: exchanging salt for cod, trinkets for fish. I have never looked back.

I knew from the very beginning that I would never know love; that my life must carry on untainted by that folly. Some whispered it must be a fault in my stars; yet I guessed the unsearchable riches that I had already earned. True, I would never know the loving embrace of a wife or have little children dancing at my heels. I would always be somewhere on the outside, marching on through the wilderness, beating my own path in the snow.

Thousands of miles west of home, alone in the Gaspé peninsula, I found my kingdom. Here I am director, shareholder and controller; here I reign omnipotent. I am scarcely a man of the Book; my labour is my only prayer. Yet a childhood Scripture often slips unbidden into my mind. 'And I will give thee the treasures of darkness, and hidden riches of secret places'.

Even now, as my commercial empire spans continents, and funnels back the riches that build the great cod-houses of Jersey, little has changed. I shun the company of others, for friendship can only make you weak. I spit at the trappings of wealth, for indulgence leads to stupor and complacency. I especially despise the sly laziness of my nephews, who doubtless will grow fat and rich off the toil of my back, using the passport of my name. They remain my only heirs.

At the mouth of Percé harbour there stands a famous rock, hewn high and strong. In winter it becomes landlocked, as the bay freezes down to the foreshore. It is blasted by the wind, smashed by the angry seas, but it prevails. I have become that rock.

*   *   *

Long ago, when the first Jersey fisherman came to the Grand Banks, the sea was thrashing thick with fish. They say a man had simply to cast a net, and the net was soon filled to bursting. News of fortune travels fast. So, the Jerseymen, the Guernseymen, the West Country sailors and the Malouins all swarmed in together, battling for the prize of the cod fisheries. By the time I set to sea, the prime fisheries of the Banks were taken, so I travelled in deeper, scouting for fresh ground, fertile opportunities. And here in the remote fisheries of the Chaleur Bay, I found them.

Needless to say, I was not alone in my quest. Others scented the same cod-stench of opportunity. How, then, did I prevail in this war of all against all? Some say it was because I am a Jerseyman, and my fluent French gives me the upper hand in my dealings with the fractious Acadian settlers and the provincial government at Québec City. Others say it must be easy for me, with no wife to satisfy or heirs to groom. Naysayers brand me as miserly and scheming; more generous souls might see me as prudent and conservative in my dealings.

The truth is simpler. I choose to work on Sundays while others pray. I choose to winter here through the bone-numbing ice of Paspébiac, while other shipmasters lounge by their St Aubin firesides. That of course means I can secure the early advantage and trap the first fish of the season.

So often, I have chosen to walk alone. Once I tramped three hundred miles through the ice for an essential assembly in the City of Québec. I was already forty-three by then, a man of advancing years and aching limbs, but my burning desire to reach the city was enough. The snow blinded me; my hands withered in the cold. On the return journey, I fell through the river ice and almost drowned. Yet I made it to the distant city, and presented my case, and forged relationships that have since earned me a king's ransom. That is the secret of my fortune; walk my path if you dare.

Others may have a venture, a business, a family tradition; but they all harbour a secret weakness. They may be dragged down by cloying domesticity, or over-zealous religion, or impatient ambition, or simple homesickness. The malady may vary, yet the symptoms of distraction amount to the same. They say in the wilderness, that when a hunter chases two rabbits, he will surely catch neither one.

Others have occupations or professions; I am become mine. The pungent stench of the cod fishery is my breath of life. As such I can never be deterred, never be broken, or lose heart. 'Let them have dominion over the fish of the sea', says the Book of Genesis, and I have followed that command to the letter.

When the American rebels burned my staithes and my warehouses, and I lost everything, I simply carried on. When the seas erupted in open warfare and French ships stole my precious cargo – for my fish are worth more than the vessels they are conveyed in – I did not abandon my mission. Last year, Spanish armies swooped down into Portugal, and all my trusted markets were blocked, so I simply scoured out new ones.

The game to me is everything, and I set out to win. Like a python smothering its prey, I ruthlessly squeezed out all of my rivals. I secured firm legal title to my foreshore fisheries and then persuaded the authorities to block all others who would dare. I have cajoled favours and peddled influence. I have flattered and tipped the ear of officials, orchestrated elections, and seen my every rival fail. I have crushed each and every one like apples in the cider press.

The local fishermen here are utterly dependent on me; I am the sole supplier of essential goods here on the peninsula and I will provide them only in return for a season's worth of fish. They are practically my indentured labourers, toiling to fill my ships. I build my own vessels, hire my own carpenters. In the spring I will send out a fleet of cod-ships to Spain and earn a rich harvest by the fall.

I have seen them all off; my rivals and contenders, the might of foreign pirates, the American revolutionaries and the power of the French navy. They have all fled back somewhere across the grey ocean, and yet the name of Charles Robin survives, and the work of my hands shall endure. The sea is mine, and all that is in it.

A day is coming soon when I will cast my bread upon the waters, and come home, back to the memory of that Jersey fireside, far across this cold ocean. I will be a silent old man soon, looking west and remembering, thinking only of the empire that I ruled and the price that I paid.

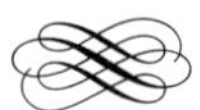

The Battle of the Oyster Shells:
A Gorey Story

The spectacular success of the cod fisheries changed the landscape of Jersey. Grand and opulent 'cod houses' were built on the back of Newfoundland money, and busy shipyards studded the coast at Gorey and Havre des Pas. The turbulence of the American Revolution was not only a disruption to the transatlantic cod trade; the Island itself was in the firing line. Jersey was invaded by a French army in 1781, and only a battle in the Royal Square saw off the invaders.

Throughout the Napoleonic wars, Jersey stood as it had since 1204, heavily fortified yet perilously exposed, perched on the frontier of clashing empires. Only fourteen miles of shallow water separated Jersey from the heart of Napoleon's burgeoning empire. Philippe d'Auvergne, the spymaster of Prince's Tower at La Hougue Bie, found it an ideal vantage point to semaphore to his network of secret agents embedded in the Cotentin.

With Napoleon's final defeat at Waterloo, the Island's fortunes changed again. The restored Bourbon kingdom of France was now at peace with the victorious British Empire. And yet the resources of the sea once again proved a bone of contention, one that would stretch relations between the maritime powers to breaking point. More than that, they would threaten to incite open revolt in Jersey itself. This, then, is the curious tale of the Jersey oyster wars.

François Godfray
Constable of St Martin
April 1838

In the wilds of America, they called it gold fever. A few years past, deep in the Georgia hill country, a scavenger unearthed a great nugget of gold. Soon enough, thousands came swarming into that wilderness; the shrewd and starry-eyed, wealthy adventurers and lean urchins, honest men and swindlers. All of them were magnetised by desire, seeking the fountain of easy riches. Virgin land was torn up in weeks, and fortunes were won and traded away in the blink of eye.

In Jersey we swooned under the self-same malady. Whereas, as befits an Island, our own precious treasure was plucked from the sea. It is the common oyster. Some may find it a little slimy and brackish, and it is certainly less pleasing to the untrained eye than a fleck of gleaming gold. What, then is its mysterious secret? Well, its taste is sublime; it practically sells itself by the brimming bucket load. One fact matters above all: London loves it, and London will pay.

As with so many fortunes, this one was spawned by chance. During the chaos and turmoil of the Revolutionary Wars, a Jersey fisherman stumbled upon a great prize. Somewhere to the north of Chausey, he landed upon a rich bank of the golden molluscs. Things were falling apart in those days; French royalists and Jacobins were at each other's throats, and d'Auvergne's web of spies combed Normandy stirring up trouble. In the anarchy of the times, the oyster reefs that fringed the Cotentin lay ripe for plunder. So, the Jersey fishermen harvested them mercilessly, and soon enough, word spread like wildfire. Men say there is nothing so discombobulating as the sight of a friend growing suddenly rich. Before long, the chartered oystercatchers of Kent and Sussex spied an opportunity to share in the piracy. They descended on Jersey like wasps to a honey jar.

The little port of Gorey blossomed. In my childhood days in St Martin, there were just a few cottages here, nestling in the shadow of the tumbledown castle of Mont Orgueil. Suddenly the port became a veritable boom-town, bursting with new shipyards and building-sheds. Three hundred fishing boats crammed into the harbour, and even the mighty new pier was not long enough to shelter them all. The cries for the States of Jersey to fund an extension became as predictable and regular as the winter storms. Without a doubt, the harbour was bursting at the seams. One and a half thousand oystermen, in a flotilla of smacks from the Medway and the Channel coast, had joined in the great plunder.

The secret of our oysters may be the taste, but out of the water, this will soon fade. Time is of the essence; they must be packed and shipped by first light. The crates are whisked off to Essex and Kent, where their salt-tang mellows in the estuary, and are sent at last to sate the insatiable appetite of London. A thousand women from the poor eastern parishes were soon toiling here in the packing stations, preparing the cargoes for export. It was manna from heaven. The poorhouses of the eastern parishes emptied, and there was a task for every hand.

Success proved to have many fathers, and the States smiled on with its benign eye. We all grew fat as oysters on the tax revenue. When the cholera came, six years back, the States even bestowed two hundred pounds to build a new church, with services in the English language, for naturally the newcomers understand not a word of Jersey French. Despite the epidemic, business boomed. Just four years ago, they were still hauling in three hundred bushels a year, the bounteous fruit of the sea. Then came catastrophe. The fishery collapsed.

And this fact explains why a man such as I, whose natural habitat is the plush Royal Court chamber, addressing the Jurats, Rectors and Constables, am in fact sat aboard the States cutter on this unusually chilly April morning, heading out into the freezing fog.

*　　*　　*

To be fair, trouble had been brewing for a long time. In times past, the French fishermen had been content to live and let live, but the rapacious industrial harvesting of their banks broke that pact. My fellow Jerseymen had conjured up the dragon of retribution.

Back in 1821, the King of France's military vessels had seized some Jersey oyster smacks and hauled them off to Granville. Their crew were brutally beaten and threatened with the gaol cell. Chastened and intimidated, they slunk back to the Jersey shore. Serious fighting erupted again in 1828, as the Jersey industry boomed. *The Times* of London reported that an English boat had been seized by French warships. Yet the Gorey fleet was not so easily beaten. When news reached Jersey, the fishermen set to sea as a war party, to retake what was rightfully theirs. They brought the recaptured English boat home in triumph.

It was a Pyrrhic victory. Jerseymen had died, and others languished in chains. Above all, a minor local fishing dispute had been catapulted into the court of international political relations. The London press barely troubled their pages with any news whatsoever from the Bailiwicks; this incident proved an embarrassing exception.

The Bourbon kings, having learned nothing and forgotten nothing, soon fell from the pages of history. The house of Orléans assumed the French throne; yet their robust maritime policy changed not a jot. They knew, and we knew, that the oyster banks were rightfully theirs. They understood that the British government, having sacrificed blood and treasure to secure the victory over Napoleon, would hardly reopen the bitter scars of the past for the sake of a few oyster shells. Peace and amity between nations was hard won but easily squandered, and a gaggle of cantankerous Jersey fishermen could not be allowed to threaten it. The Crown barred them from the banks.

Peace and amity. I rattle those words around my head as we approach the craft in the bay. I can see them now. Any sympathy I have with their hardship dissipates as my cutter draws closer. We spent a king's ransom seeding this part of Grouville Bay, to establish an alternative supply for the oystermen, but the bank is delicate, and like a field left fallow, needs to rest undisturbed for now.

The greedy fishermen are plundering it like pigs in a trough, scraping the rich seam of oysters, filling their boots up like thieves. It is time to put an end to this madness. The authority of my office will bring them to heel.

Then I hear a sound over the waters: a mocking, spiteful chorus, calling out my name. There are hoots of derision, chortles of laughter. A few gestures of the utmost vulgarity and insolence follow in short order. The fishermen are jeering at me.

*   *   *

Constable Godfray, scion of one of St Martin's most illustrious families, celebrated orator and member of the States of Jersey, had been openly humiliated. He made swift moves to arrest the ringleaders the next morning, but like the mythical serpent, the rebellion simply grew new heads. On the tenth of April, he begged the Royal Court for help, but they refused his entreaties. Dismayed but unbowed, the Constable would be forced to appeal over their heads.

As the icy morning of the twelfth of April dawned, a flotilla of fishing smacks already sat out in the bay, plundering the oysters once again. These were men who had openly defied French gunships; why should they be dissuaded by the blustering father of the parish? The answer would become clearer as the day unfolded.

The Constable, it transpired, had powerful friends. In the early hours, even as the fishing boats set out to sail, a detachment of the British Army is already assembling in the Royal Square. Their mission is clear: to crush the sedition, by any means necessary.

*   *   *

The time has come to scare these vagabonds out of their wits. These are regular soldiers from the Fort Regent garrison, the 60th Regiment of Foot. They are men of the King's Royal Rifle Corps, posted here from Winchester for a season, who care little for the Island and its curious, impenetrable parishes. The rural fiefs of Jersey feel like a land of foreign tongues and unfathomable feuds. The Rifles will soon put a silence to their bickering.

The Rifles are supported by the St Helier battalion of the Jersey Militia. These were townsmen, English speakers for the most part, with few loyalties or blood ties with the Jersey fisherfolk of the eastern parishes. Should bloodshed ensue, their loyalty would be assured. To put the eventual outcome of any skirmish beyond doubt, the soldiers are towing behind them a battery of artillery. Four heavy guns; that will suffice.

The cold April sun bursts out over the bay, silhouetting the swarm of boats that is dredging the oyster beds bare. The Lieutenant-Governor, Major-General Archibald Campbell, surveys the theatre of war from the wintry heights of Mont Orgueil now. He stands on the battlements of Raleigh's ancient castle, clutching his bronze spyglass and peering down upon the splendid bay. He's a wizened veteran, who fought with honour long ago in the Peninsula Wars. Today, instead of the cream of Napoleon's armies, he is facing a gaggle of truculent Jersey fishermen.

Still, this is a seething age of revolution, and hunger proves itself the father of many a crime. Weakness will be sniffed out and a decisive response, he thinks, is necessary. Some say the fate of Britain itself hangs like a fragile looking glass, in the hands of its uncrowned eighteen-year old queen.

The Lieutenant-Governor's cannon are ready to fire.

*   *   *

April 12, 1838
A Jersey Oysterman

It's a bright morning out here on the bay, and God knows we need one after the winter we've endured. In these last few years, the fisheries have been whittled away like wood. Our children cried out for bread, and our own bellies ached with the cruel needling of hunger. This has been a cold, hard time.

We've watched the age of prosperity unravel before our eyes. Saturday afternoons used to be a celebration, when the oyster fleet hauled home with our catch, and the English agents crammed into the 'field' to barter for them at high water. Men of Kent, Portsmouth boats and Shoreham smacks jostled with us in the bay, and lines of women and children snaked along the shore, drenched in brine, bringing the baskets in.

Those bounteous days are gone. The first stirrings of trouble came when the foreign ships started to challenge us on the banks. Suddenly our boats were being seized by the French navy, and crews were hauled off to Granville. Some of my friends spent their summer locked in irons. A few of them lost their lives. At least, we thought, the British government would defend us, and rescue us from this foreign intimidation. We were wrong.

Then came the bombshell from London: that a limit of two leagues would apply. If we neared the French coast any closer, Her Majesty's ships would leave us to our fate. At a stroke, our prize beds were stolen from us and delivered into the hands of the Granville fishermen. Our livelihood was cut from beneath us. The States vainly blustered and protested. but were forced to obey. The vaunted liberties of this Island counted for nothing.

Most of the English boats left for better pastures, but we sons of Grouville could hardly abandon our parish. No longer did the shipyards of Gorey ring with hammers. The town had fallen silent. Saturday was a wake, as we hauled in with a meagre catch and empty baskets, our children wailing for food and our purses bare.

Some men continued the night fishery, braving the danger of French chains. The rest of us timid souls waited for the States' own oyster fishery to be established. Seeing the calamity on their doorstep, they voted a great sum to seed the beds and save our jobs. Then, in a cruel twist of officialdom, they barred us from using it. Their gift has been hedged with so many caveats, so many restrictions, as to be a poisoned chalice. Until one day last week, we decided to claim that which we are rightfully owed.

Thunder is breaking now, rolling in heavy and deafening over the bay. There are flashes of lightning somewhere by the castle. But the skies are curiously bright. Then the water around my boat explodes and I am thrown to the deck. It takes all my strength to keep the boat on its keel, to avoid a capsize.

As if in an astonishing dream, I watch a barrage of cannon balls smash into the water, then flame up in vast waterspouts of fire. Someone has unleashed the gates of hell. The bastards have opened fire on us.

Revolution, as they say, suddenly holds all the appeal of a damp squib. We are sitting ducks here in the bay, and this is no time for hotheads or hare-brains. The oyster rebellion is over. In dribs and drabs, my fellow oystermen are already running back to shore, preparing to give up the ghost. I curse, spit, reach for my tiller and follow them home.

*   *   *

The fishermen deemed it a miracle; for no-one was actually injured in the bombardment. Given the fearsome accuracy of the British Army's artillery, the Lieutenant-Governor had clearly decided that a warning volley would be sufficient to bring the renegades to heel. No-one wished to see another Peterloo massacre; the mere show of strength would be enough. They were proved right; for the fishermen proved cowed and penitent and swore never to rob the oyster banks again.

The mood soon turned for the better when most of the oystermen were immediately released on bail, and the detachment of soldiers was regaled with gifts of bread, beer and cheese, before they returned to barracks. In the end ninety-six of the errant boat masters received fines, and only two ringleaders were thrown into the cells. The 'Battle of the Oyster Shells' was over.

Jersey's oyster industry was wounded; despite fits and starts, and some further cycles of prosperity, it would never regain its crown. The gold-rush of the glorious early days would never return, and all of the shipyards would be gone in a generation. Constable Godfray, having wisely decided to seek election as Deputy in a friendlier parish, would go on to serve thirty-three years in the States and live to see the industry's decline. Eventually, the Battle of the Oyster Shells became a mere curiosity, a tale of passions raised and dashed, a plate photograph of a strange and fleeting moment in Jersey's history. The new Queen visited Jersey in 1846, and gradually the Hungry Forties gave way to the optimism and prosperity of the Victorian age.

The Battle of the Oyster Shells did however claim one prominent victim. Jersey's ageing Lieutenant-Governor, worn down by the exertions of this cold day, had caught a sudden chill. His health took a regrettable turn for the worse, and the finest oysters in Jersey could not restore it now. Within a month, Major-General Campbell, victor of the battles of Vitoria and Grouville Bay alike, would be dead.

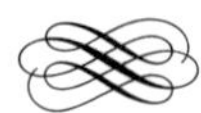

Autumn

AGE OF PLENTY

Inside the Fairy Palace:
The Great Exhibition

The world is changing. Prince Albert, the scion of the Victorian age, puts it best – 'the unity of mankind is within reach'. Technology drives his optimism. 'The distances which separate the different nations and parts of the globe', he declares, 'are rapidly vanishing and we can traverse them with incredible ease; thought is communicated with the rapidity, and even the power, of lightning'. The telegraph, the penny post and the maritime arteries of empire are binding the world together, and Jersey is deeply enmeshed in the web. Indeed, the first pillar boxes in the British Isles will open in St Helier in 1852.

To celebrate the new era of global seaborne trade, the Prince Consort has called upon the world to showcase its greatest treasures in London. They call it the 'Great Exhibition'; and Jersey and Guernsey will occupy a prominent place.

Colonel John Le Couteur
Hyde Park, London
1st May 1851

An emissary from the future has landed at Hyde Park, and Queen Victoria is riding out to greet it. This crystal cathedral is an extraordinary glimpse of tomorrow: an astonishing ice palace, carved from nine hundred thousand square feet of glass, rising out of twenty-six acres of prime London parkland.

As a proud Jerseyman and aide-de-camp to Her Majesty, it is an honour to witness this day. I stand here at the opening of the 1851 Great Exhibition: a visionary project to showcase the finest works of human and natural creation. Prince Albert, its instigator and architect, says it will provide 'a living picture of the point of development at which the whole of mankind has arrived', and a worthy inspiration for further innovations. He has struck the mark.

I can scarcely imagine that six million people – over a quarter of the population of Great Britain – will be mesmerised by the show before the year is out. Every nation has shipped its most exquisite works here, vying to showcase the most sublime craftsmanship, the fastest machinery, the most serene art. And Jersey and Guernsey, as the Crown's oldest bailiwicks, occupy a prime position at the very heart of this magnificent new Crystal Palace.

As the Exhibition opens on May 1st, thirty thousand visitors cheer the young

Queen. Secrecy has shrouded the great project for months; behind barriers, two thousand men and four steam-pumps have toiled away unseen. We could only imagine the marvels that they had conjured. Now the veil has at last been lifted, and the astonishing scale of the works are revealed to the world. The Exhibition occupies almost a million square feet, and the galleries alone stretch for almost a mile.

The immediate sense of light and space proves somewhat alarming, and many visitors are left dizzy, unsettled by the shock of the new. The official Catalogue will note a 'sense of insecurity, arising from the apparent lightness of its supports as compared to the vastness of its dimensions'. Even the original great elms from the park have been incorporated within the glass, like strange arboreal specimens from the past, their arms brushing up against the soaring ceiling. At the Exhibition's hub stands Osler's Crystal Fountain – a translucent masterpiece shooting twenty-seven feet of water. It is built from four tons of pure crystalline glass, and the world has seen nothing like it.

Queen Victoria advances to declare the Exhibition open, to the strains of the National Anthem. I am lost in a sea of dainty bonnets and tall stovepipe hats; one onlooker amidst the tens of thousands overawed by this feast of treasures. After all the cheering, there is a profound silence, as we recite the choruses and prayers. Thirty thousand voices abruptly fall still, and I feel as if I am falling into a deep well.

The Archbishop of Canterbury concludes his address. As Handel's angelic 'Hallelujah' chorus resounds throughout the cavernous palace, I have a strange sense that we stand present at the creation, at the start of something profoundly new. We have been granted a glimpse of the world to come.

The Queen departs. As if the heroes of History itself have come to pay homage to the future, the ancient Duke of Wellington follows in her train. The poor old chap looks very feeble, but still he touchingly offers a supporting arm to his old comrade and sparring partner, Lord Anglesey. The two grand old men survey the miracles unfolding all around them. Instead of cannon fire, they walk into a battery of spontaneous and heartfelt applause.

Truth be told, so many of us had feared the opposite – an angry republican mob, or worse. The shadow of the Hungry Forties is not so long past after all. Yet the worst transgression I witnessed today was from an enthusiastic royalist, who had shinnied up a high platform to catch a better view of the Queen. He was soon ushered down with an indulgent smile. Far from some towering Babel of confusion, this Exhibition seems the very model of decorum and order. The crowds swarm, like bees; bustling hither and thither, but in a sentient and ordered fashion, churning out the sweet honey of Progress. I have a season ticket to the building and will visit again and again.

As the weeks go by, I am delighted to note that the peace and order continues even on those days when tickets are cheapest. In fact, the gentry, shelling out their half-crowns for plum viewing times, are not nearly so polite as the ordinary Londoners.

The exhibits are marshalled into four categories – Raw Materials, Machinery, Manufactures and Fine Arts. The world's treasures have been corralled here: from freshly mined California gold to the Koh-i-Noor diamond, glinting enticingly from behind its Chubb security cage. Yet, in my opinion, the industrial wonders surpass all. Electric telegraphs even enable us to summon carriages directly to the gates to meet us – no need to wait in line for a hansom cab!

When I was a young boy, a galloping horse was our fastest carriage. Now we behold locomotives that can devour seventy-three miles in a single hour. Imagine my own joy and surprise as I tested a wonderful new quill that actually holds a reservoir of ink inside it – and it writes beautifully. No more need to scrabble around in inkwells after every second stroke! Mark my words: they call this device a 'fountain pen', and I believe it is going to make history.

*   *   *

Colonel Le Couteur was not the only visitor who left thunderstruck. The Great Exhibition seems to have sparked euphoria in many; a sheer intoxication with the power of technology. The great writer Charles Dickens himself visited twice but withdrew, overwhelmed by the dizzy kaleidoscope of sights. Yet for most, the house of wonders proved as hypnotising as the recent California gold rush. It was quite simply, in Colonel Le Couteur's words, a 'fairy palace'.

The Great Exhibition was the fruit of the vision of two men of unbounded and immense energy – Henry Cole, reputedly the inventor of the Christmas Card, and thirty-one-year-old Prince Albert himself. The objective was Utopian – to foster global peace, to beat swords into ploughshares. In the Channel Islands, poised on the front line of clashing kingdoms since time immemorial, the message was well received.

Colonel Le Couteur overcame his initial misgivings and decided to embrace the project. He would eventually visit the Great Exhibition no fewer than fifteen times. In his capacity as a scientist and founder of the Royal Jersey Horticultural and Agricultural Society, he personally exhibited over a hundred specimens of wheat from his gardens in St Brelade. Seven of them proudly bore the name 'Jersey'. Mens' and Ladies' Committees in both Islands were established, and parish Constables even called house-to-house to seek funds.

After a short display in Gloucester Street in St Helier, the exhibits were shipped to London, with Henry Cole, the effervescent dynamo behind the Exhibition, personally escorting them to their stand. Jersey and Guernsey occupied an enviable position on the north side of the nave, next to Ceylon and India, near the Crystal Fountain at the centre of proceedings. The red saltires of Jersey hung majestically above the stand, with the leopards of both Bailiwicks prominently displayed on flags above.

The stand, built by George Clement Le Feuvre and William Stead, was designed to showcase the beauty of the Islands. It featured a plentiful array of traditional woollens. There were decorative shells from Herm and samples of Guernsey Blue granite, the stone used on the steps of St Paul's Cathedral.

Jersey butter-making was also demonstrated daily during the Exhibition. Le Couteur recorded in his diaries that one churn produced 21 lbs 2 oz of butter in just two minutes, and another churned 28 lbs in just four and half. The latter portion he gifted as tribute to the Queen, and he personally called at the Palace the next day to ensure it had been safely received.

A Channel Islander provided one of the greatest technological marvels of the Exhibition. The crowds were mesmerised by Guernseyman Thomas de la Rue's 'Patent Envelope Machine', which occupied its own special display. In a series of elegant and balletic mechanical moves, it cut, folded, gummed and forwarded thousands of envelopes an hour. The machinery was astoundingly productive, and as graceful as a swan, yet it was operated just by two boys.

One Jersey work of art was even honoured by an illustration in the official 1851 Great Exhibition catalogue. While lamenting that 'the contributions from our fellow countrymen in the Channel Islands are comparatively few', it praised 'a CHEFFONIÈRE, or sideboard, manufactured by Mr G C LE FEUVRE, of Jersey; it is made of oak, a portion of the wood being the produce of the island; the designs in the compartments are worked in tapestry'. The emblems of England, Scotland and Ireland adorned embroidered panels, sewn by Mrs Le Feuvre.

The upper section of the cheffonière depicted King John, surrounded by rebellious barons and bishops, poised to sign the Magna Carta. One bishop wields a patriarchal cross; another bears a mitre. Alas, this section did not meet the Catalogue's refined critical standards, so was not deemed worthy to be illustrated. Still, Jersey's local woodworkers had gone head-to-head with the world's pre-eminent artisans and had proved their worth.

The Great Exhibition shone like a supernova burning in the sky, drawing the world to it for a season. Yet the fairy palace that shimmered at daybreak would not last. This glittering temple of materialism finally closed its doors in October 1851. After six months, it was relocated to the heights of Sydenham in south-east

London, where it would eventually burn to the ground, in a darker, sadder century. The charred remnants were swept aside, along with the hopes and dreams of the Victorian age. Only the name endures.

Yet the Exhibition was a signpost to the future, fulfilling the extraordinary prophetic vision that Prince Albert had decreed in his original speech: 'The Exhibition of 1851 is to give us a true test and a living picture of the point of development at which the whole of mankind has arrived in this great task, and a new starting point from which all nations will be able to direct their further exertions'.

Albert would die tragically young, but he left us Albertopolis, the extraordinary cultural wealth of South Kensington's museum quarter. His golden statue presides there to this day, clutching the Exhibition Catalogue. Inspired by his legacy, little Jersey would go on to hold the Channel Islands Great Exhibition in 1871 at the Victoria College Showground.

Yet as the Great Exhibition at Hyde Park closed its doors in 1851, the triumphant Le Feuvre and Stead faced a more prosaic dilemma on returning home to Jersey. They had incurred substantial expenses in the project; how best to recoup the funds? It was strictly against Exhibition rules to sell the display products, so they devised a lottery.

The first prize would be the ornate cheffonière itself, valued at the princely sum of £350. Alas, the States of Jersey took umbrage and intervened to scupper their plans. The Lottery was cancelled. So, what became of this exquisite piece of craftsmanship, viewed by millions, and arguably one of the most celebrated works of art in Jersey's history? It appeared to vanish without trace. Some say it still stands somewhere in a grand English house, holding fast to its secrets, a story waiting to be told.

*   *   *

The Great Exhibition sparked an age of creative ferment. In London, the upstart painter Millais, who hailed from an old Jersey family, was fomenting a revolution. In 1852, he completed his masterpiece 'Ophelia', and ascended to the artistic pantheon. Decades later, his touching invocation of Jersey's most famous Governor, 'The Boyhood of Raleigh', would earn its place as a lodestone of the Victorian age.

Back in the streets of St Helier, Philip John Ouless was rapidly establishing his own more modest reputation as Jersey's foremost marine artist. He pioneered the eerie new technology of the daguerreotype from his studio in Royal Square. His well-to-do subjects took a leisurely seat; then the alchemist weaved his magic, and somehow, on a silvered copper plate, he spun out their exact likenesses. The 'photograph', it seemed, was the shape of things to come.

A year after the Great Exhibition, Ouless painted one of his most famous seascapes, the 'SS Amazon on Fire in the Bay of Biscay'. The subject matter was compelling; a wooden-hulled paddle steamer that had recently encountered ruin on its maiden voyage from Southampton. The ship was a tinderbox; stuffed to the brim with barrels of coal and bales of hay. Fatally, it also carried five hundred bottles of mercury bound for the mines in Mexico.

Somewhere, west of the Scillies, the ship ignited. The fire was cataclysmic, and over a hundred souls perished. Ouless's masterpiece reveals the sheer power of the inferno; the ship's funnel glowing red-hot in the night, a lifeboat slipping away over the fiery waves; and the cold moon hanging pitilessly above the scene.

Ouless became a prolific maritime artist, and Jersey provided a rich canvas. The Island thrived in the Victorian heyday of empire; as a tax-friendly retreat for retired colonial administrators, and a sun-drenched escape for holidaymakers. The healthy seaside air of Havre des Pas proved an ideal tonic for those who dwelt in the soot-blackened, choking industrial cities of Britain. As newcomers and visitors flocked to St Helier, the old town grew. Ancient fields were replaced by streets bearing English names; côtils were consumed by the expanding townscape, with only their shadows remaining.

Regular steamers plied their familiar path from Southampton to St Helier, and the character of the Island changed. English was now the undisputed lingua franca of the bustling town, with the traditional tongue of Jèrriais pushed back into its rural bastions. Jersey developed a voluble anglophone press to cater for the needs of its new denizens.

The commercial heart of Jersey remained its harbour, which in the early days of Victoria's reign extended up to the Southampton Hotel, with boats moored just in front of the Royal Yacht Hotel. Sir John Coode's ambitious plans for a grand deep-water harbour foundered in the face of insuperable technical complexities and the weeds of political infighting. Eventually, after the squandering of a small fortune, the New North Quay would be completed, and the top of the old harbour filled in.

The oyster industry, whose violent passions had fuelled the drama of the 'battle' of Grouville Bay, had long since dwindled and faded. Before long, the Weighbridge heaved in season with a new treasure: potato carts and crates, feeding England's insatiable appetite for its produce.

At the height of the Victorian age, Hugh de la Haye, a Mont Cochon farmer, picked up two freakishly giant potatoes from Lecaudey's stores on the Esplanade. They were bulbous curiosities, deemed unworthy for export. In those days, 'La Grande Charrue', or Great Plough, was an important farming gathering; at one of these, Hugh dismembered his potato into fifteen or so pieces. When planted, they yielded a golden harvest of succulent kidney-shaped offspring. The Jersey Royal had been born.

It is now the Spring of 1886. Queen Victoria is nearing her forty-ninth glorious year on the throne, and the ageing William Gladstone is embarking on his third ministry. In New York, the pedestal of the Statue of Liberty is being completed; in France, Gustave Eiffel is promoting his radical designs for a quite astonishing tower. Yet as the new year dawns, Jersey finds itself in the grip of turbulence, of a banking crisis. Hard on the heels of the Jersey Banking Company's collapse comes the shocking news that, as a result, the storied Charles Robin Company itself has been plunged into bankruptcy.

In these unsettling times, it is curious that the tragic story of an ordinary Jersey girl gripped the imagination of Jersey press and people alike. Yet the unsettling tale fulfilled so many of the sensibilities of any Victorian narrative, offering original sin, a damsel in distress, a dramatic court trial, a terrible ordeal and a surprising deus ex machina *resolution. Yet this quintessentially Victorian tale belongs in no penny dreadful or Dickens periodical. It is the astonishing true story of Miss Louisa Journeaux, a guileless young lady from St Clement.*

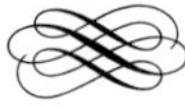

Louisa's Story: Into the Night

April 1886

"We are all just a slip away from oblivion. Any of us can fall in an instant. Consider our dear neighbour: a precious young lady, a churchgoer no less, who paid a terrible price for a moment's madness. She placed her very life, her trust, into the hands of a young man she barely knew, and he threw her into the abyss. Remember her fate tonight and pray for her soul".

The preacher wielded his words like sharpened knives, letting their echoes clatter down onto the flagstones. Every syllable cut deep. The congregation cowered, recoiling in shock, for they knew this tale all too well. The whole Island had grieved for a month now, speaking of little else save the heart-rending story of Miss Louisa Journeaux, of St Clement's Parish, presumed dead.

Louisa's tragedy was the shame of the Island, the anguished lament of newspaper correspondents, the daily prattle at the Town Pump. True, the Honorary Police were yet to find any trace of a body, merely the remnants of her pathetic, broken parasol. Yet it would surely be only a matter of time before her swollen corpse came in with the tide.

Everyone knew the dreadful mistake that poor sweet girl had made. Her final moments were known only unto God, but the outcome of the tragedy was clear to all. Louisa Journeaux would never be coming home.

Louisa Journeaux
St Helier, Jersey
Sunday - April 18, 1886

It was Palm Sunday, the day when Jesus rode his donkey into Jerusalem long ago. The promise of Easter was just around the corner, and I had bought some lovely greeting cards, showing fluffy chicks pulling fairy carriages. Unbeknownst to my younger cousins, I had also scoffed a tray of Fry's delicious chocolate eggs, but I would be sure to replenish my supplies before the Easter Egg Hunt itself.

My cousin Julia and I had dozed dutifully through Evensong, but it was such a beautiful evening, that kind of clear Spring day in Jersey when the sky is simply ablaze with colour. It seemed far too early to retire to bed. True, I am twenty-two years old now (whisper it softly!) but Julia and I are still feisty little girls at heart; we simply fancied another adventure.

After church, we strolled down through Royal Square, where we had seen all those handsome and dashing soldiers on parade – it must have been five years ago – to mark the centenary of the Battle of Jersey. Of course, this being a Sunday evening, all the shops were boarded up now, their shutters drawn down. The brash advertising hoardings advertised the fine merits of Perrot's print-shop to just a few passing pigeons. And as we walked down past the Public Library, a peal of gorgeous birdsong burst all around us.

It promised to be a glorious sunset. We soon broke out onto the Weighbridge and were greeted by a forest of tall masts. It seemed to me that each one was whispering salt-tanged promises of faraway harbours, and every ship had a secret to share. My heart began to sing.

Caught in this haze of delight, we were strolling down to the waterfront with our parasols, when two young Frenchmen caught our eye. They were larking around near the Westaway Memorial, dancing right in front of the railway terminus, and with typical Gallic bravura, they brooked absolutely no delay in introducing themselves to us.

The eldest I recognised at once; M. Jules Farné, a young gentleman I had already laughingly conversed with a few times at the shop counter. He was a dapper hairdresser with a wayward smile and an accent that soon enough melted my heart. *"Would you like to join us for a drink of cocoa?"* He regaled us with delightful tales of Paris; of Spring in Montmartre, of artists and cherry trees, and the astonishing ice-white basilica they are apparently building there, high above the city. I was hooked like a fish.

His best friend, M. Radiguet, who was a little less bold, lavished his courtly attentions on my cousin Julia. We all laughed and joked together, and shared steaming cups of hot chocolate as the rays of the evening sun lapped down over the Weighbridge. Perhaps they dropped a dash of some French liqueur into our drinks; who can tell? The night was balmy, and the moon was rising high above the Fort. Then suddenly a madcap notion darted into our evening like a sparrow falling in the square.

Jules proposed it so flamboyantly, so poetically; and I was at once bewitched. "Let us take to the water", he told me. "Let us drink in the moonlight together. It is the French way. I will be your captain, your brave pilot at sunset. I will take you out upon the waters, and then I will lead you home".

*   *   *

Channel Approaches, West of Jersey
Tuesday - April 20, 1886

The raw anger of the Atlantic slams with the force of a cudgel against Louisa's matchstick boat. She is thrown hard by the shock of the breaking wave, and rolls like a rag-doll across the timbers, grasping at them for sheer life. She is too numb to cry.

Louisa is far from home now, dozens of cold nautical miles away from land. Stripped of its oars, her little skiff is casually tossed by swells the size of hills; is cast like a child's wooden toy over a sea-crest, then spins away to float gently in its sluggish wake.

In these brief moments of respite, Louisa finds herself working like an ox, despite her utter exhaustion, to bail out the saltwater that is slowly drowning her craft. She scoops it out with Jules Farné's hard felt cap, the last reminder of the would-be lover who left her to die.

The Atlantic Ocean is an unforgiving place, where sky and sea merge, and gut-churning swells drench and batter her boat. Yet there is a strange beauty in this void. In the icy stillness of the night, the stars hang as close and bright as lanterns, blazing across the skies from pole to pole. No-one else is here to witness the astonishing sight.

On her first night at sea, Louisa briefly glimpsed the Southampton steamer cutting up the horizon; since then she has been utterly alone.

Everything in this world is drenched to the core, corroded by a seamless curtain of sea and rain. Her dainty ladies' parasol was lost in her first night on the water; now she faces the second night with no shelter at all. Louisa's Sunday best, her church finery, are mere sodden rags and a heavy chill has started to gnaw into her bones, turning her legs to lead.

Louisa's raging thirst is slaked only by mouthfuls of rainwater, but she is still feverish, driven to delusion by the pummelling tides. Somewhere deep inside, Louisa is preparing to die. Her thoughts are flying away with the seabirds across the black ocean, and her mind is slowly turning as numb as her hands. For a fleeting moment, she half-remembers the comfort of her father's cosy fireside; but tonight, her home feels as distant as the icy moon.

* * *

A sorrowing pall of grief hangs over that childhood home, Elder Cottage in St Clement. No-one in the Parish can forget the shock of that awful first night when her cousin Julia returned; shrieking like a demented banshee, and alone. Neighbours clucked behind curtains when the Centenier rode by at daybreak; now parishioners cross themselves in sympathy as they pass the smitten house. Louisa's ageing parents are cloistered within, riven by grief, confined to their beds. As news spreads, a pulse of anger is seething across the Island; more than a handful of hot-tempered young lads are already thirsting to beat Jules Farné to a pulp. To keep the spectre of mob rule at bay, the wheels of Jersey justice are grinding forward with unaccustomed speed.

By now Jules, the sometime rowing boat captain, is impounded in the St Helier police cells, in the stern custody of Centenier Le Gros. He had been found clinging like a limpet to the pier-head, half-drowned and blathering. Under police interrogation, the facts have started to tumble out like a haul of fish; slippery, evasive and thrashing with obvious contradictions. Yet with the help of the distraught witnesses and with the shadow of the gallows lurking in his fearful imagination, the authorities slowly gather a clearer picture of the night's tragic events.

It had all begun with such an innocent fancy. Jules confessed he was desperate to romantically impress Louisa, and despite his sketchy nautical skills, he was confident he could capably handle a little rowing boat in a sheltered harbour. So, the young Frenchmen hired skiffs from portly Mr Du Feu; Louisa and Jules would share one of them. The boat-keeper warned this was foolhardy, that night would be falling soon, but the youths were bothersome and insistent, so he reluctantly trousered their coin.

It was already a quarter past eight, and the dying sun was slipping down behind Noirmont, when the two skiffs finally slipped away from their moorings. At first it was a jaunt, a sheer lark, punctuated by giggles and banter. Louisa and Jules began to drown in each other's eyes. At sea, any prying gossips would scarcely see the couple nudging dangerously closer. The sky glowed a soft and gentle pink, with dark blue cotton-clouds painted as if by hand onto the golden sky. Seagulls cawed and circled overhead.

They soon made the pier-end, but caution be damned: the water was as smooth as a millpond. It was an unseasonably humid night and Jules, drenched in perspiration, loosened his tie a little and unbuttoned the upper buttons of his shirt. The skiff glided silently across the water, and Louisa was soon hypnotised by the rhythm of the oars. He would give her one last adventure, he promised. He would race out to the Castle and complete a final glorious circuit under the moon, then ferry her safely home.

The last magical lap at sunset unfolded in a shared dream. Louisa was besotted with this oarsman's skill; he was clearly no novice. Then the first stars nuzzled out from behind the night-clouds, dancing a chorus of blessings. Jules pulled the skiff back into the embrace of the Victoria and Albert piers. Now was the time. He swung both oars in, boldly grasped her milk-white hand and moved in ever closer, drawing her towards a moonlight kiss.

'Then I saw that there was a way to hell, even from the gate of heaven...' As he did so, his concentration lapsed. The first oar slipped from its rowlock and splashed noisily into the harbour. Jules swore in French and attempted to turn the boat, but he was fumbling and distracted, and the second oar followed it under. The tide was now ebbing fast out to sea, tugged by the magnetic pull of the moon. The moment called for action. Jules deftly leaped into the sea to chase the oars, but emerged spluttering like a fish, empty-handed. He tossed his felt cap back into the boat, then vanished. The tide was relentless now, and his screams were lost in the rising darkness.

Louisa was gone. Her boat was hurtling away fast on a brutal ebb tide. She screamed back – for Jules, for help, for deliverance. No-one came. She screeched again, until her throat was blood-raw and her eyes stinging with tears. No-one heard. Then the glittering lights of St Helier receded as if in a dream, with the Weighbridge lamps a last painted flourish of yellow in a canvas that was fast rolling up behind her.

Within minutes, the landward horizon was a smear of black coal, and the last points of light had utterly faded. Louisa was viciously dragged out to sea by the raw power of the tides, as if tied to a runaway horse, or carried away on a locomotive with no driver. Stinging drops of rain started to pelt down like daggers. She raised her flimsy parasol to counter them, and it shredded in minutes. Then everything faded to black, and her bearings dissolved in the darkness. Her world had shrivelled to the sodden innards of an open boat. Her last cries muffled by the rainstorm, and far from any shore, Louisa fell away into the night.

*   *   *

The Royal Court was packed to the gills on the day the prisoner was dragged in for his trial. The Crown's formal charge struck the young man with the force of an oar to his skull. Jules Farné, had 'by his neglect and imprudence, caused the death or disappearance of Louisa Journeaux'. A parade of witnesses was called forth to testify. A broken parasol had been found washed up on the rocky headland at La Collette, and Mr F. Journeaux formally identified it as belonging to his beloved daughter Louisa. The press summarised his testimony: 'Last Sunday his daughter attended divine service, and afterwards went for a walk. He did not know the accused; but was aware his daughter was acquainted with him'. Then Miss Julia Wiltshire, dressed in black, gave her own solemn account of the fatal rowing trip.

The rival Advocates jousted like medieval knights, sparring with brutal parries, rhetorical lunges and the occasional chivalrous flourish. The prisoner had given two separate, conflicting accounts; but Advocate Le Gallais, defending, maintained that the whole thing had been a deplorable accident. His words carried weight. In the end, the Magistrate determined that there was insufficient evidence to convict the accused. Jules Farné had failed miserably in his duty as a gentleman, but no foul play had been proven, and, above all, the search had yielded no body.

Silently, and under the withering stare of the Constable, Jules Farné was released from the cells in the early hours. All eyes were on him, following him down the street, waiting for an opportune moment to intercept him. So, he sprinted down to the docks and fled on the first ferry to France, just one step ahead of the wolves.

Public interest, verging on hysteria, remained high. A letter to the British Press and Jersey Times *lamented that laws on prohibiting skiffs to roam outside the harbour would be somewhat fruitless 'in these liberty-loving days'. Yet Victorian ingenuity and practicality offered a better way: the writer proposed 'an efficacious remedy… every scull must have a lanyard made fast to it just inboard of the rowlock. By this simple arrangement, an oarsman could never lose his sculls, even if he tried to'.*

Truth to tell, few had come out of this tragic episode with much credit. The young ladies had been foolishly naïve; the Frenchmen reckless albeit not criminally culpable; the boat-owner rather too keen to pocket coin on the Sabbath. Much criticism also centred on the shockingly sluggish speed of the official rescue operation. It was a full day before the Duke of Normandy *tug boat steamed round the coast, hunting for signs of a rowing boat, or timber wreckage, or a sea-bloated body.*

All efforts failed; every search drew a blank in the vast labyrinth of the seas. In desperation, soldiers dynamited the sea-bed between the piers, but the muffled explosion dredged up only a tangle of fishing nets and some timbers from an old wreck. There was no sign of the young lady who had rowed here at twilight on Sunday evening. Louisa had been swept off the face of the Earth.

Prayers went unanswered; headlines moved on. In Elder Cottage, grief festered deep in the bone. The weeks slid by. And then came a knock on the door. An urgent telegram had arrived, from across the face of the globe.

Louisa's Story
St John's – Crown Colony of Newfoundland
May 1886

God rescued me, and I will never know the reason why. I was no Grace Darling, giving up my brave life to save mariners. I was certainly no Nightingale. I was just a foolish, reckless girl. I had spent my last breath of hope, and accepted my inevitable fate, when I first saw that ship steaming towards me. I had no strength and no voice left; I had only my sodden pocket handkerchief to wave. It was enough.

As if in a dream, the great vessel came alongside and threw me a rope, but I was far too weak to grab it and the ship sailed on by. *Tombold* of St Malo, its stern proudly read; a French Atlantic steamer.

So, the sailors turned back and rescued me. They carried me like a child, deep into the bowels of their ship. Captain Edouard Landgren, my hero, my second father, had saved my life. He ushered me to a modest cabin and to me it was as welcome as a royal palace. He offered me a set of his own clothes, which were mercifully dry if (I confess) hardly flattering for a twenty-two-year-old lady! He plied me with sweet cider (which I refused) and strong hot tea (which I lapped up); but I soon collapsed into a deep and dreamless sleep. I woke to find the cabin lurching like fury around me. Soon after they found me, the ocean had erupted into a savage storm. I had been plucked from the maw of the beast.

The violence of the weather prevented any hope of return; we were unable to change course but ploughed on for some two thousand three hundred miles across the Atlantic. The voyage was long and bitter; some three weeks into the journey, one sailor was swept overboard and drowned in the deep. Yet the French sailors treated me ever so kindly, as if I was an honoured princess aboard their ship. Twenty-six long days and nights later, the shores of the North American continent hove into view, sheer cliffs shrouded in a thick peasouper that reminded me very much of home.

They tried to moor in the French fishing grounds of St Pierre and Miquelon, but the fog prevented it. So, they ducked in to the tiny fishing harbour at St George's, where the Rev Jeffrey and his wife welcomed me in. The sun burst through at noon. As fate would have it, it was another beautiful Sunday afternoon when my rowing expedition across the Atlantic Ocean finally came to its appointed end.

And so today I am seated in a small bureau in St John's, the colonial capital of Newfoundland, observing a most curious and beautiful device. It is an incredible instrument, resembling a piano keyboard, but with twenty-six keys, one for each letter of the alphabet. Spinning behind it is an electric motor and rotating mechanical drums, like some mesmeric creation from a Jules Verne novel. They say an undersea cable runs from this very room, thousands of miles across the ocean to Valentia Island in Ireland, thence to London, and finally over to Jersey. It feels like an umbilical cord calling me home. The Colonial Secretary has ordered a telegram to be sent to the office of Her Majesty Queen Victoria herself.

This is the machine that sent my story to the other side of the Earth. This is the device that told my Father that I am alive. Now it will tell my family that I am coming back soon, across the great divide, and that soon enough I will see their faces once again. Before the summer is out, I will stand on Jersey soil.

The machine is ready now, whirring with the strange power of electricity, pulsing with the hope of tomorrow. Then the operator reaches for the keyboard, and silently begins to tap my message home.

*　*　*

Louisa Journeaux was safe; a survivor who had endured the raw power of the ocean and had lived to tell the tale. Captain Landgren was feted and presented with a gold medal at the Town Hall, but Louisa shunned the attention. She settled down to a conventional life, working in a draper's store in St Helier, and she would live to a ripe old age.

Louisa may have stood in the limelight for a season, but the nineteenth century proved to be an age of extraordinary women. Many Jersey ladies broke through the restrictive shackles of social convention and dared to achieve greatly. One of them trained to become the first female medical doctor that Jersey had produced, but her ambitions did not stop there.

This lady journeyed to the ends of the Earth not for gold or glory, but to preach the Word, to help the poor, and to heal the sick. In doing so she travelled to the hidden heart of an ancient civilisation that was just beginning to reveal itself to the world. Her name was Dr Lilian Grandin, and this is her story.

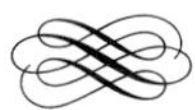

Lilian's Story: Into the Heart of China

Regent Road
St Helier, Jersey
1905

China. The name burns like a diamond in my mind. I was born in St Helier, in a house above the railway cutting. As a child, I would gaze up at the red granite cliffs of Fort Regent, dreaming instead of the soaring towers of the Great Wall. Whenever shabby steamers crept into Victoria Harbour, I glimpsed ocean liners docking at the Bund. Then I would watch the toy-town trains puttering out from Snow Hill station, down into the suburbs, like dreams slithering away to die. I was not born to dwell here in Jersey, my horizons caged in by the sea. I yearned for something else, for enough adventure to last for a thousand years.

So, even as I studied diligently in the brand-new halls of the Jersey Ladies' College, my heart was already stolen. At night, I gorged on the telegrams from Shanghai that filled the columns of the *British Press & Jersey Times*. They opened windows into another world; a beguiling tableau of opium and opulence, beauty and death. China haunted my dreams, a sea of souls calling me in the night. Deep in the forgotten interior, the reporters said the human need was desperate. Few Westerners dared venture within, least of all women. "Here am I, Lord", I whispered in the night. "Send me."

My father encouraged me to follow my calling. He had raised me as a Bible Christian, a church that recognises women as equal partners in the kingdom of heaven. I was one of six daughters, after all; my two little brothers had fallen victim to whooping cough. My mission was only to see that no-one else need die.

Edinburgh has been training lady doctors for thirty years. So as soon as I graduated from the Jersey Ladies' College, I headed to study for a full degree in medicine. I devoured dentistry in Scotland, midwifery at the Rotunda in Dublin and specialised in eye diseases at Moorfields. The final course was a dose of studies in tropical medicine. I stashed up a full larder of knowledge to give me sufficient strength for the road ahead.

They say this journey will be hard, even bitterly so. I shuddered when I leafed through the histories of the martyrs. I was still a medical student when the appalling fate of Reverend Chalmers at the hand of South Pacific cannibals electrified England. I wept at my desk for him but was galvanised by his sacrifice. For the Scripture reads: 'Be thou faithful unto death; and I will give thee the crown of life'. We all face the inevitable grave, but it is what we achieve in the days before that really matters.

We were warned time and again: the Chinese Empire is a tinderbox, waiting to explode. Stay in the treaty ports; do not venture deep into the interior. Yet I still yearned for the diamonds in the night, the field of souls calling me home.

I made my irrevocable, public declaration at my church's 1905 conference. The hall was spellbound, and tears welled in the congregation's eyes as I consecrated myself to the mission field. *"I would now dedicate myself for work in China. It is not easy, but I go in God's name."*

A warm cocoon of applause enfolded me. Yet I trembled like a lamb as I stepped down from the stage, into my Father's arms. That night, I wept right through until morning.

*   *   *

Yunnan Province
Chinese Empire
Winter 1907

Nothing can prepare you for China. They call it the Celestial Empire, the Middle Kingdom, the vital centrifuge of the world. The rest of the globe is spinning in orbit around its centre. Yet even when we finally reached the foot of the Gorges, a thousand riverine miles from the coast, we found we had barely penetrated its heart.

I said my final farewell to Jersey at a valedictory service at Great Union Road Chapel. The gentle grey cliffs of the northern parishes faded like a sorry smudge on the horizon as the steamer pushed north, and then they were gone. The waters of my life had parted, and the former things had passed away.

We left Southampton on the *Princess Alice*, a German ship heading for the Suez Canal. The journey was languid, as we steamed down through the tropics, by the teeming cities of Imperial India, and at last docked at the treaty port of Shanghai. The city proved astonishing, a hotchpotch of West and East. The Bund glimmered with a cluster of elegant towers, quite as impressive as Glasgow or Liverpool. This was the shiny skin of the apple. We were to burrow deep into its core.

When we boarded the *Lui-Wo*, a smart little river steamer, it felt as if we were about to take a mere holiday jaunt up the Yangtze. Its sky-blue decks dazzled invitingly in the sunlight, and the yellow river glimmered in the sun. And we glided upriver into the empire, as if falling into a dream.

It was a delightful surprise to meet a fellow Islander amongst the crew. Mr Good, the Chief Engineer, is from Gorey, and he fondly remembers the days when the flanks of the castle rang with the hammers of the shipyards. I asked if he had ever returned home, and he only smiled. Once you have crossed the line, he replied, there is no easy way to go back. In time, he said, I will come to understand.

Mr Good may be an old China hand now, but even he did not sleep so easily in the night. Safe passage was far from certain. We heard rumours that a posse of Boxer rebels had slaughtered a group of Catholic priests like lambs. I prayed for strength and mercy as we drifted to sleep in the boat.

Yet the voyage was uneventful, and we finally drew into the great river port of Hankow. We were hundreds of miles upriver and we were no closer to unveiling the secrets of the real China. We were still mired in the dismal world we knew, of international treaty ports, Western concessions, and the gospel of Free Trade.

Hankow's sky is inked black from its factory, which they say is the only steel-rolling mill in the whole of China. They make guns here; a hundred Mauser rifles a day, and much else besides. The plume of black smoke twists up above the works like an ominous dragon in the sky. Yet despite the industry, the streets are largely unpaved, half-waterlogged in the winter rains. Locals insisted that a sedan-chair is essential for any respectable traveller. Yet the luxury sat uneasily with me. Crowds stared at me, as if I was some sort of curiosity, a peacock on display. I arrived at my lodgings winded and uncomfortable from the journey.

Soon enough, we pressed on deeper into the interior. The villages and towns whirled by in a tapestry of colour and at last, at the river-port of Ichang, our river-steamer reached its final port. They call this place the door to the West. Beyond these blue mountains, we would discover the real China.

We push on into the Gorges, into an older, darker world. The miasma, the dank breath of the river, seeps into everything. Wood rots and decays; cockroaches thrive. This is an ancient land of bamboo fields, of windmill palms, of farmers toiling relentlessly in conical hats; the China of my childhood imagination made flesh.

Seven men sleep here on the nose of our boat. The night passes in a shivering darkness; the days are sly and humid. We glide past perpendicular walls of rock a thousand feet high; the miraculous has become familiar. Hauling the boats over each set of rapids is a blisteringly harsh operation, requiring a cast of hundreds to overcome the brutal energy of the river and push the boats on upstream. The trackers that ease us over the rapids look like famished wraiths of men, scraping to earn a few pennies. Occasionally, the captain tells me, a river-man will stumble and lose his footing, and the river will devour him.

I scream at the shock of the impact: we have hit a rock. A surge of river water bursts over the boat and drenches my dress. Then the crew bundle us all onto a marshy bank, and we shiver like rats. The captain is haggling fluently with a local Kwei-fu carpenter, and for the princely sum of five shillings, he agrees to repair the craft.

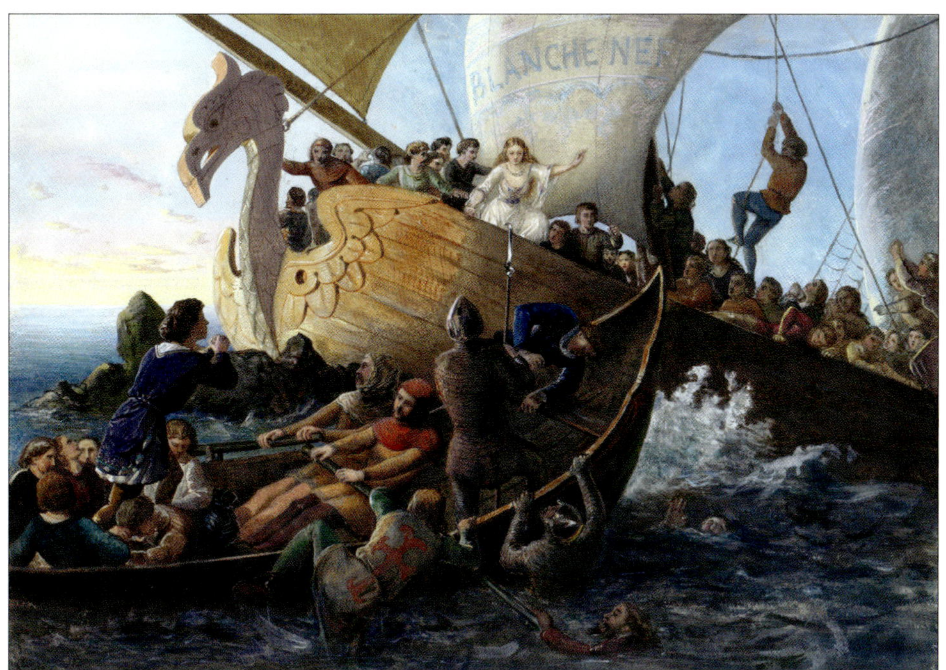

The Wreck of the Blanche Nef (1866) by Princess Louise, Duchess of Argyll (1848-1939). Royal Collection Trust/ (c) Her Majesty Queen Elizabeth II 2019

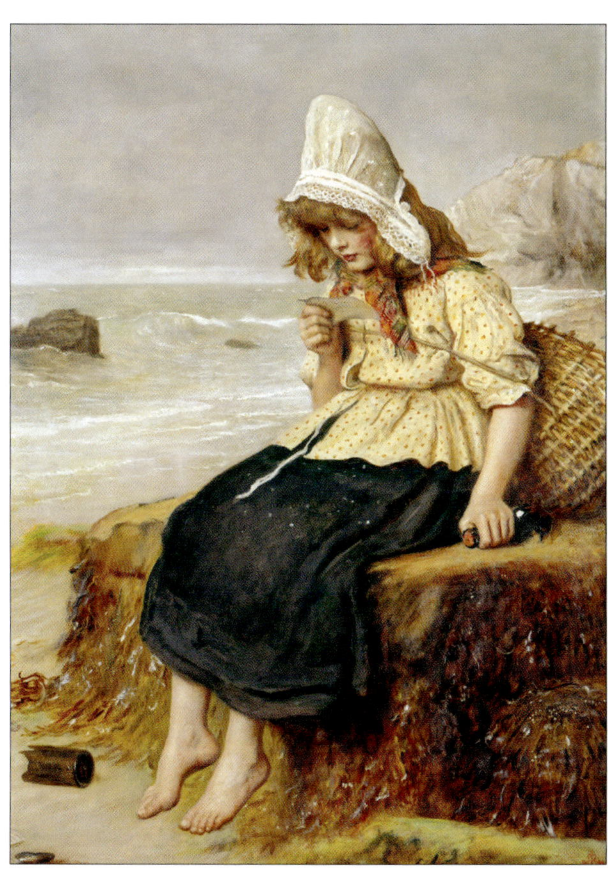

A Message from the Sea (1884) by Sir John Everett Millais, Bt (1829-1896)
© Medici/ Mary Evans

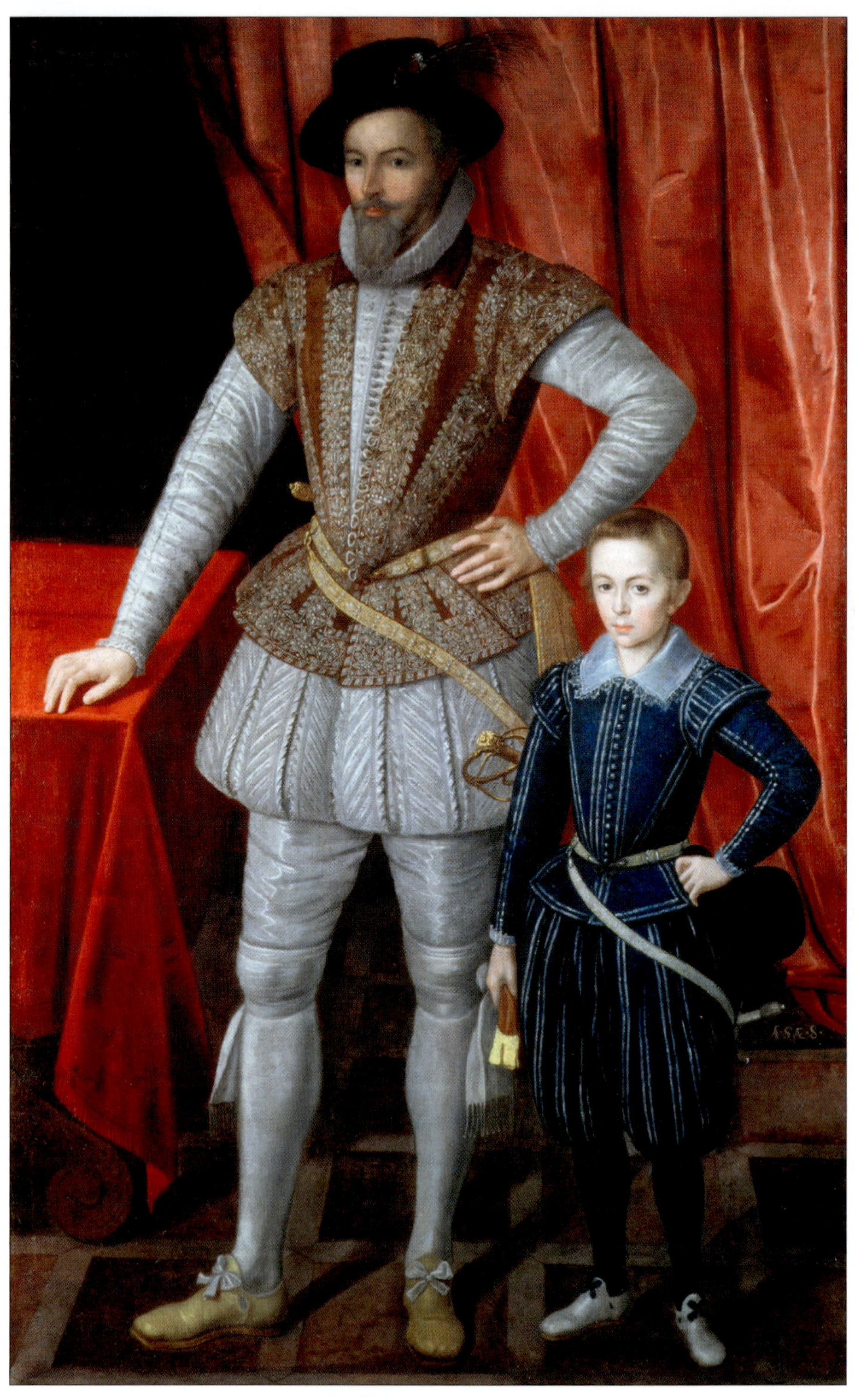

Raleigh and his son Wat
Sir Walter Ralegh (Raleigh); Walter Ralegh (1602) by Unknown Artist
© National Portrait Gallery, London

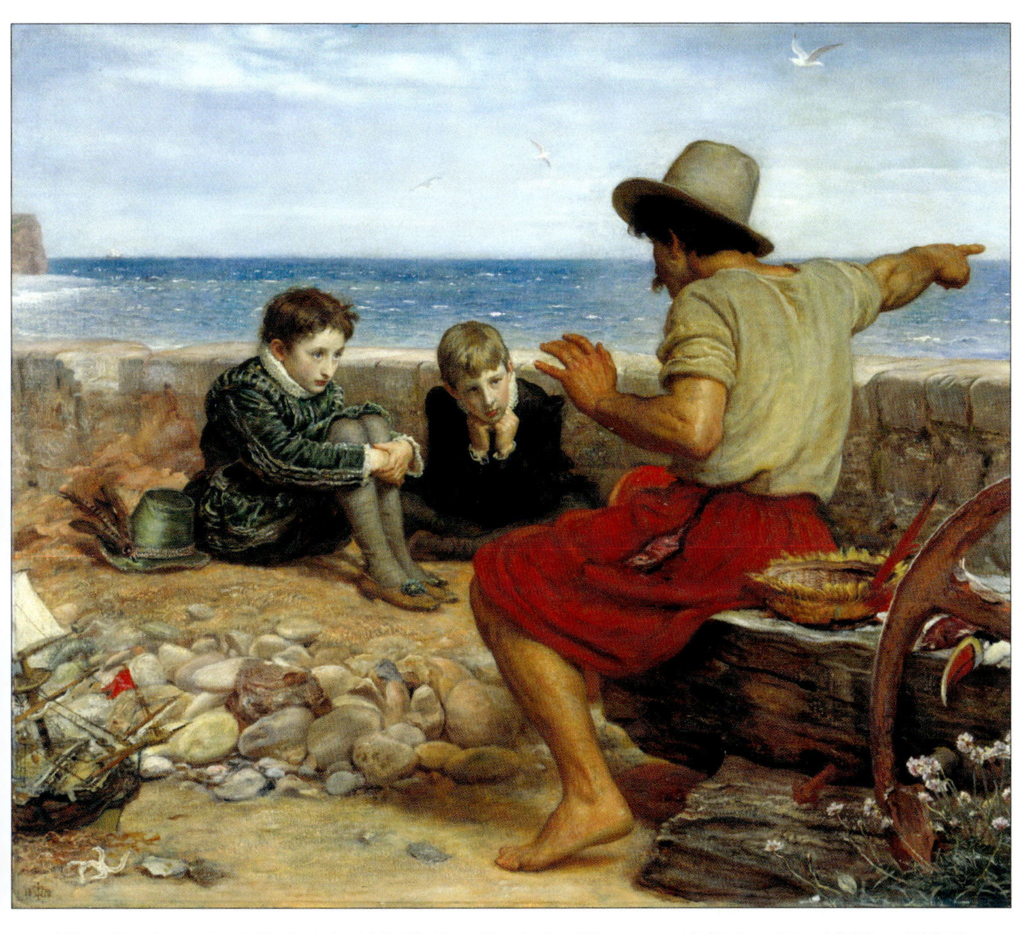

The Boyhood of Raleigh (1870) by Sir John Everett Millais, Bt (1829 – 1896)
© Tate, London 2019

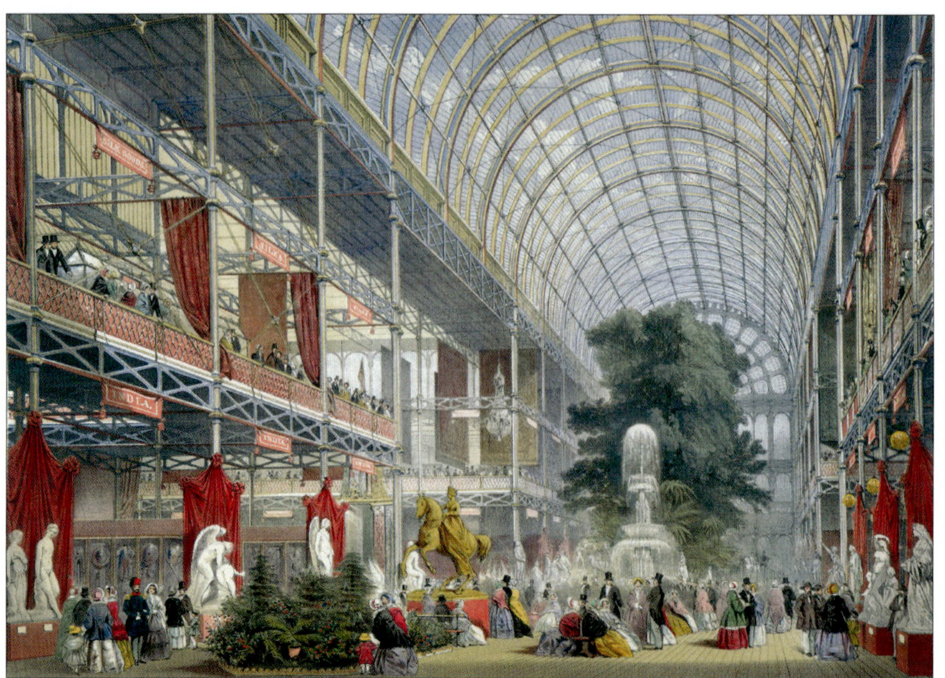

The Great Exhibition of 1851

The transept, inside Crystal Palace, Hyde Park

Image taken from Dickinson's comprehensive pictures of the Great Exhibition of 1851. Originally published/produced in 1854. © The British Library Board. (Cup.652.c.33 volume 2, frontispiece)

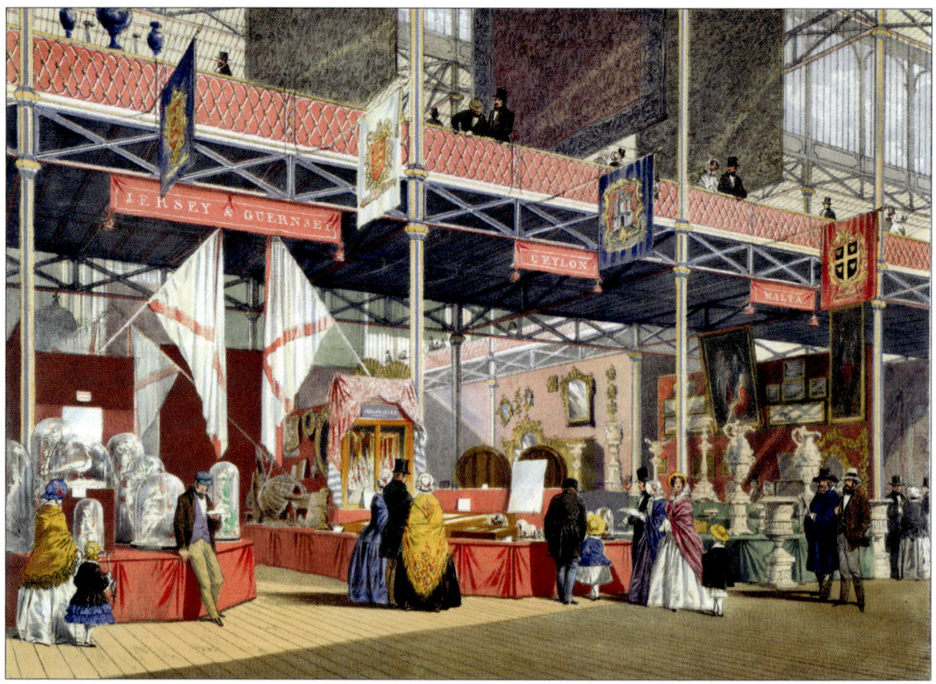

An exhibition gallery representing Guernsey and Jersey, Malta and Ceylon

Image taken from Dickinson's comprehensive pictures of the Great Exhibition of 1851. Originally published/produced in 1854. © The British Library Board. (Cup.652.c.33 volume 2, plate X)

I expected a remedy of tar or pitch; but he proceeded to caulk the seams with a stew of beef suet and flour. Astonishingly, the curious seal held firm, and we proceeded upriver. Only at last, when the upper reaches of the rapids became utterly impassable, did we reach our final moorings.

Our last week was spent on horseback, trekking deeper into the mountains that would soon become my home. The seasons have turned again now, and the noon-day sun grills us like pigs on a spit. When night falls, we sleep in our overcoats, lodging in the cheapest rooms, where the walls crawl with insects.

Yet the land we pass through is as beautiful as a dream. The mountains rise like jagged diamonds, impossible peaks straight from the poems of Coleridge. Every square inch of flat ground is a precious rarity and is duly cultivated. Gorges collapse in on themselves, tumbling away thousands of feet without warning. A single slip would mean death. Caves bristle with stalactites, forming grotesque faces in the shadows. Then waterfalls spring above us like blessings, breathing rainbows.

At last the mountain city of Chao-Tong gleams on the horizon. This is the old walled city where I will work and live, perched some six thousand feet above the sea. The iron gates of the city swing open, for we have long been expected here. The world is almost medieval, frozen in time for a thousand years. Peasants toil beneath the Empire's watchtowers. There are no electric lights or steam-trains at all out here, and the skies blaze with clear stars.

Poverty is written into the landscape here, like a forlorn poem. Children are clad in rags, their limbs marred by lice-sores, running in the gutters. Dogs snarl and fight in the streets. A clutter of street vendors offers me monkey-nuts, marrow seeds and even the exotic rarity of a Nottingham cigarette.

A bell tolls mournfully for us, as if welcoming home the dead. Two gaunt shadows stand before us, like ghosts in the night. They are Dr Savin and his wife, waiting for us at the gates of Mission House, and tears are welling in their eyes.

*　　*　　*

The mountain country is as large as France, and I am the only qualified doctor. There are no paved roads here, and the roads become quagmires in the winter rain. So, I bought a little black pony for the equivalent of two pounds ten shillings, and laughingly dubbed him the 'Black Prince of Rozel'. This little fellow has become my salvation. He is my motor-car, my steam-train, my only carriage, winging me across backbreaking mountain roads to the remotest of settlements. I smile whenever I call for him, my beautiful smidgeon of home. Jersey is just a fading memory now, somewhere I carry deep within my heart.

The outlying villages of Yunnan province are cursed with leprosy. Old men proffer claws for fingers, shrivelled and blackened. As my Master instructed me: "Go out quickly into the streets and alleys of the town and bring in the poor, the crippled, the blind and the lame". So, we invite them all in, clean them from lice, and offer them comfortable quarters.

I am raising a devoted army of Chinese nurses, and they toil on with unrelenting dedication in the wards. Yet the human need is incalculable. I meet orphans with emptiness in their eyes, and grey-bearded men shuddering as death draws them tightly to itself. In our little hospital, the sickly groans of the bedridden mingle in a terrible choir with hammering cholera coughs. This is my church now; I am home.

All my childish fantasies of spiritual glory have been shorn from me. There is nothing left for me but brutal routine, and the cage of exhaustion, day after wretched day. The losses inexorably mount. I feel as if I am Sisyphus pushing my rock up the hill each morning and collapsing in a pool of sweat upon my bed every night. Here on the mountain, I have carved my own exquisite prison.

In winter-time here, they perform Chinese theatre, tales crafted from lanterns and darkness, stories of melancholy and shadow. They say the puppets, if not dismantled and boxed correctly, will come to life at night and haunt the town. I sometimes believe they are already standing amongst us. Exhausted, I scan the rare newspaper from home, weeks out of date, an echo from a distant star. The world beyond these walls seems to be falling into shade, pulsing with revolutions and rumours of war. I have come to see that we are all shadow puppets, pulled along on strings, acting out our parts in the play.

*   *   *

With the 1911 revolution, China at last emerged from the long hibernation of the Imperial Qing dynasty. Lilian's work in the mountains continued unabated, far from the seething turmoil of the cities. And even in her lonely mission at the roof of the world, love would not elude her.

Edwin John Dingle, spiritual seeker, journalist and intrepid Chinese adventurer, was the man who won her heart. He was the first Westerner to immerse himself in the life of a Tibetan monastery and chronicle his astonishing journeys by foot across the interior of China. The couple slipped back to Jersey to marry in 1912. Then the darkness fell, and during the turmoil of the Great War, the missionaries were withdrawn. Afterwards the inevitable work resumed, through poverty and revolution, until the day was done.

In the end, the people of Yunnan would remember Lilian Grandin as the 'Angel of

Zhaotong'. Her grateful patients even compared her to the legendary founders of Chinese medicine. Her little hospital proved a lifeline for a province of a million people, when there was nowhere else to turn. Lilian was there when the rains came, and the mists of autumn fell upon the valleys, and when the maize harvest turned poor.

It was 1924. Autumn turned to winter, and brutal floodwaters rose, bringing a typhus epidemic in their wake. In her last letter home, Lilian confessed the difficulties were mounting, but she would carry on the work. Her faith alone would sustain her. 'Well, we know the Reservoir is unsoundable, so there is no need to be downhearted, is there? And we are not so'.

The typhus epidemic swept in with the winter rains. History records that Lilian gave away her very last vial of medicine, to save the life of a Chinese patient. It was a deliberate act of self-sacrifice. And on the fifth day of December, Lilian went home. The news of her death filtered back slowly at first, a thousand miles down the river, reaching the editors of the 1925 Report of the United Methodist Church Missions (Home and Foreign) just before they went to press. The hurried tributes praised her 'experience, adaptability, her generosity'; a worthy addition to the book of martyrs. She was forty-eight years old.

Time passed. The little weather-beaten house on the railway cutting in St Helier was forgotten. Within a few years, the train line closed at Snow Hill and the station was shuttered forever. Edwin Dingle had relocated faraway to Los Angeles, where his esoteric teachings soon found a ready audience in the boulevards of Hollywood. During the Great Leap Forward, even Lilian's gravestone in Yunnan province was dismantled and used for building materials. She slipped out of living memory.

Yet eventually after the long winter, the cherry blossom flourished. The ordinary people of Yunnan had never forgotten Lilian, and in time her grave was lovingly restored. Today, in a China utterly transformed, her legacy remains. A well-appointed hospital of two thousand beds stands on the foundation she laid. Her mission church is thriving. In the timeless shadow of the mountains, Lilian's work has endured.

In Jersey, they planted a Chinese gingko tree in her memory at her old school, breaking out its roots and carefully transplanting it to the new Jersey College for Girls building at Mont Millais. It is a living memorial to the Jersey girl who once dreamed she could play her part in the healing of the nations. The tree is growing strongly, and many unborn generations will walk in its shade. Some even say that the gingko tree can last for a thousand years.

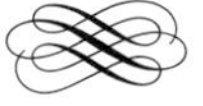

Elinor Glyn:
Jersey's Queen of Hollywood

*L*ilian Grandin's journey had taken her from the cosy domesticity of Regent Road, St Helier, to a sacrificial death on the far side of the earth. She was not the only feisty and single-minded Victorian Jerseywoman who set out to claim the world. In the year she was born, two sisters were growing up just a few streets away, in an unhappy house that reeked with the stench of gin.

The odds were stacked against them as they began their journeys, but through fierce determination, both Lucy and Elinor would leave their mark on the twentieth century. Their paths would eventually take them from that dreary house on Colomberie to the glittering catwalks of New York and the sun-drenched boulevards of Hollywood respectively. But that would be in the century yet to come.

Wind the clock back, long before the cascade of fame and wealth, and you will just find two frightened little girls, on a black steamship, heading home in the night. Winter has fallen hard, and a shroud of fog cloaks the Channel as the overnight ferry trundles down from Southampton to St Helier. The hours of the night have dragged on, and landfall cannot be long. It has been an uneventful voyage so far, but history has other plans.

SS *Havre*, en route to the Channel Islands
Platte Boue Rocks
16 February 1875

Like many a marriage, the ship broke without warning. It was a violent, rapid sundering, a splitting of shinbone and calf bone as the old vessel skewered itself fatally onto the rock. We were all jolted awake by the impact, as if the sea and earth had fallen in beneath us. The loud reverberations juddered and screeched through our cabin, like the bellow of a harpooned whale.

I was a wilful, wayward girl of ten on the day we collided with the rocks. We were on our way back home to Jersey, back to my island prison. My desperate mother had taken me with my elder sister Lucy for a week's parole in London. The trip was a disappointment. As a child, I had dreamed of a fairy-tale city of hale and hearty burghers, of noble streets paved with gold. The vicious squalor of London told a different story. Everything there was choked in black; soot-flakes swirled around us as we left in the black winter fog.

Our carriage rattled back down to Waterloo, whisking us past the fetid rookeries of Seven Dials. Desperation lurked here, in the broken palms of the street beggars, in the sad eyes of the flower-girls plying their trade on every corner. Nothing good could remain here unsullied. Nothing beautiful would endure. Still, for a precious few days we were at least free from the tyranny of our step-father. The days fled. Then from Southampton Docks, we slipped back onto the dismal packet steamer that would ferry us safely back home.

Many a slip betwixt cup and lip. Eventually the ship's lacerating death-rattle subsided, replaced by a low, resigned growl. The hull had breached. Within seconds, a violent surge of black water spilled right through the cabins, breaking into our quarters like a thief. Sheer instinct took over. My mother roughly pushed us up the gangway ladder, half-dressed, out of the suffocating womb of the boat onto the icy deck. I wheezed and rasped my cries, my breath raw. The winter spell had broken.

Women shrieked in their nightclothes in the freezing February morning, some nursing whimpering babies to their breasts. I heard one of the crew agitatedly shout that the engine room had already flooded. The ship was lost. Then panic broke out. In the half-darkness, I saw a couple of ferret-like men, rifling through other passengers' abandoned bags, brazenly seizing the opportunity to steal and pilfer. In the chaos, a rich man's purse spilled open, and a shimmer of half-sovereigns and silver sixpences cascaded across the deck. Slowly, as if in a dream, I watched his coins slip away into the oblivion of the black and angry sea. It scarcely mattered in our strange new world, for everything had changed.

Scuffles were now breaking out on deck. Some young militia boys, whose discipline had fled at the first glimpse of terror, had barged their way onto one of the lifeboats. A whiskered old colonel, his neck-veins bulging with fury, was doing his level best to stop them. "Women and children first", he yelled, "or you will face the consequences!". Even in the midst of this chaos, people stared, and despite the darkness, their glances could fell trees. Chastened and publicly humiliated, the soldier-boys sullenly backed down and let us through. The ship's officers, burly men in stovepipe hats and greatcoats, ushered us down into the wooden lifeboat. The deck had become a rising alp, with the jagged angle of a broken bone. We struggled to steady ourselves on the slanting timbers, but Mother did not let go, and our lifeboat was winched down into the sea.

We slipped away from the catastrophe, bearing across half a mile of seething, turbulent water as the lights of the sinking ship faded away behind us. As we breached the central channel of the Russel, thin curtains of saltwater broke over us. A baby wailed at the shock.

I was physically numb. The cocoon of my life had burst open. My empty life in

Jersey; my bullying stepfather, the suffocating provincial routines of the governesses and formal dinners, had just been blown apart with the force of a hurricane. A secret part of me exulted in the ravenous eye of the storm, at the rage of Fate and Fury, and the breathtaking truth that the dice had rolled, and I could not control where they would land.

My fellow passengers were silent and dressed in black, like wax effigies being hauled back to the museum of history. I fancied romantically that the gods of the red granite, the drowned kingdoms of the Channel, had come to claim us for their own, and throw dice for our souls. I felt somehow through the turbulent, lashing waves, a strange sense that all that had happened and could ever happen was flying away from me, lost in the scudding seas, a forgotten illusion.

I resolved to show no emotion. My grandmother, long ago back in icy Canada, had told me to be brave, just as our ancestors had faced the guillotine with equanimity in the Place de la Révolution. To be poised and dignified on the inevitable steps to the scaffold; that was all. The rest was in the hands of history.

Behind us, a brilliant distress flare shot up from the wreck, dancing like an angel in the night before falling to earth. It was a sublime sight, as beautiful as the fireworks display over Elizabeth Castle. A moment's false sunshine briefly enveloped our little lifeboat; revealing the snivelling children, the huddled passengers, our pilot lighting a defiant cheroot in the face of imminent death. Then the last of the bright colour drained from the skies, and the shroud of grey mist descended again.

We plunged away through the cauldron of the channel, a witch's sea-fog swirling around us and masking everything from our sight. Eventually the shipmaster moored us with great difficulty on a vicious, exposed shelf of rock and we hauled ourselves out. Drenched and shivering, we huddled like puffins on the brine-soaked ledge. The 'Grand Amfroque' the sailors called it, but it seemed doomed ground; without a blade of grass. We were outcasts, perched on a crossroads between this world and the next, waiting to find out which way we would go. The relentless incoming tide would soon answer that question.

As the tides rose, the ship slowly drowned, like an exhausted fly struggling in vain against the side of a bell jar. Baggage began to float away from it, parcels and worldly goods floating on the amber tide. A smattering of letters drifted past, Penny Reds in the sea, lost messages, their fastidious copperplate ink smeared away by the salt tide, declarations of love or income tax demands that would never reach their final destinations.

Perhaps this little girl of blazing red hair, of green gemstone eyes, would also be lost forever, my words swirling beneath the waves. The waters would close, as if I had never been. The caged songbird would drown. I could hear the vicar's solemn epitaph now. He had once thrown me a withering, sorry glance, and muttered disapprovingly to my mother that "'twas such a pity she did not have Lucy's hair". In his eyes, my unruly flame-red tresses were the mark of Cain. It was a vivid sign of social disgrace; a stigma I could never shed. Mother often threatened to use a leaden comb to make my curly locks darker, though knowing my temper she never dared.

Perched here in the numbing cold, my thoughts wandered back to home. My prison was a rented house called Richelieu; in the old French, they say this means a home of a wealthy person. My stepfather would rage for hours, the curses of an embittered old man. My young, devoted mother had remarried for duty and was soon cursed with the yoke of this petty despot. He was a rich miser, whom my mother had to beg for five pounds a year to feed her children and fund a home. He whiled away his days playing backgammon while a series of iron governesses tried and failed to tame us.

Only in my imagination would I soar, feasting on a chained library of gods and heroes, princes and thieves. There was no book step in the library, but I would grab whatever novels or poetry lay within my arm's reach, from Don Quixote to the diaries of Pepys. I drifted off during the tedious brimstone sermons at St Mark's Church. Secretly at night, I prayed to Zeus and Athena, to the pantheon of joyful and playful gods and goddesses. They promised sweet escape from this sour and petty Island, imprisoned in its iron corset of formality. I would often pity those tethered Jersey cows, beautiful creatures bound by rope, forbidden to stray, forced to feed again and again on one tiny patch of barren grass. Their ribcages poked out from their lean carcasses. I looked deeply into their sad doe-eyes and saw myself.

Above all, I dreaded the violence of the waters that swirled around my island prison. Every night I dreamed of ten-foot waves, of rising seas, of crawling to escape the incoming flood. I dreaded the secret caves at Plémont, where the capricious turn of the tide could seal you in and drag you under. Now the winter waves were surging in over the rock ledge, and my worst fears had become flesh.

Hanging here on the frozen rock, the borders of the past and future had merged, as surely as the heavy fog that blurred the boundaries of land and sea. The sullen, brutal gods were angry, and had passed final judgment. I felt no urge to escape, but simply a strange and passive acceptance of Fate. The pitiless seagulls circled high above us, but their unearthly and meaningless cries were strangely comforting. We could scramble no higher now, and the waves were already lapping at our feet. Soon the tides would claim us, and we would surely and inevitably drown.

All the frivolous Greek gods of my library at Richelieu had fled. I turned in the last back to the words my grandmother had taught me. I murmured beneath my breath a final prayer, over and over, "Gentle Jesus, meek and mild, look upon a little child." I shivered and closed my eyes.

A foghorn broke into my head. It seems that some quarrymen had noticed the flare, from the north coast of Guernsey, where they were mining rich seams of blue granite to build the new monuments of London. A ramshackle armada of schooners and fishing dinghies had been despatched from St Peter Port. I watched as if through a wall of glass as the burly sailors drew close. In the end, all hands were saved.

I often remember the rescue ship, churning through the sea-fog, a real peasouper, as stale and dank as the London smog we had left behind. We pitched and bucked on the treacherous seas, but we had felt the fury of the ocean, and lived. Far beyond and unseen, the salvage crew departed, and the packet steamer fell at last down to the Channel seabed, nestling in the drowned hunting grounds of our ancestors.

The Jersey newspapers dutifully screamed the story of the heroic SS *Havre* rescue, and soon forgot; but we could not, for we were utterly changed. Life had been revealed to us as a brief and precious adventure, to be seized and devoured. We petulant children were no longer content to be passive prisoners of Fate and social convention. We grew into forceful and ambitious young women, determined to make the future yield to our will. The world turned and our step-father died. Set free from our prison, we 'caged birds' flew.

Since that day, I have always feared and avoided the sea. I still dream every night of the vicious spring tide at La Collette, that Jersey headland where the rocks splinter and tumble down like glass into the churning bay. I am always scrambling up, outrunning my fate, heading for higher ground.

They say history repeats itself, and often has a sting in the tail. A day was coming soon when my beautiful, brave sister Lucy, at the height of her fame and wealth in 1912, would board another doomed ship, this one bound for New York. It was a mammoth and splendid vessel, the very pride of the White Star Line. But I imagine you already know the name.

*　*　*

Lucy and Elinor grew up into a pair of socially ambitious and utterly self-assured Jersey girls. Lucy, later Lady Duff-Gordon, eventually became a pioneering couturier with her own fashion house, Lucile Ltd. She would indeed survive the icy wreckage of the Titanic *disaster.*

Elinor's own life was lived in a whirlwind of energy. She was determined to escape the 'quaint and faintly pathetic little Island' of her birth. After a dizzying spell in Paris, she married Clayton Glyn, a wealthy Essex landowner and country squire. He provided her with a ready-made place amidst the landed elite of Victorian England, in a world of sumptuous country house soirées and shooting parties.

Yet within weeks of the wedding, her romantic dreams were already being curtailed by his dour country practicality. Elinor, full of the joys of spring, longed to stroll through a beautiful bluebell wood in the estate, but she was strictly denied entry lest she disturb the pheasants. Soon enough, Clayton's affection towards his young wife was cooling, and the marriage drifted into a loveless marriage of convenience.

Elinor nonetheless produced two baby girls, Margot and Juliet. Unbeknownst to her, the prospect of lacking a male heir sent her husband into a downward spiral of depression. Immediately after the birth of his second daughter, Clayton fled to Monte Carlo and burned the colossal sum of ten thousand pounds on the roulette wheel. In his eyes, without a male heir, there was no longer any point in passing a penny onto the next generation; everything must go. The family fortune was permanently destroyed in that single night of madness.

Frustrated by her husband's waning affection, Elinor's creative urges found another outlet. She penned a light-hearted portrait of fashionable society, entitled The Visits of Elizabeth. *It was an immediate sensation. In an age where women were still denied the vote, she personally negotiated the same terms as Rudyard Kipling, the leading author of the day. Her impressive advance for her second novel was £500, fortified by 25% royalties; the cash sum alone could buy a London townhouse.*

Long ago, as a young girl, Elinor had seen the legendary actress Sarah Bernhardt play in Theodora, *in Paris. Her majesty, her allure and her incredible personal magnetism had left an indelible impact. The idea suddenly occurred to her – what would happen if such an incredible, fierce woman fell in love with a dashing young English gentleman? This conceit formed the basis of* Three Weeks, *the novel that would seal Elinor's notoriety and make her fortune.*

The plot was hardly Shakespearean. A dashing and handsome young man, fresh out of Oxford, falls under the allure of a sophisticated older lady. She turns out to be a Balkan queen whose life is in danger, and for three weeks they enjoy a passionate love affair. It was hardly its language that made Three Weeks *an immediate sensation. The writing was effulgent and overblown, as the era demanded, but the content was tame even by contemporary music hall standards. In Edwardian eyes, the book's scandalous power arose from the shocking social assumptions in the novel. In this romance, the powerful woman is in complete control – she is the hunter.*

Three Weeks *was an immediate sensation upon its release in 1907. Within nine years it had already sold nearly two million copies in Great Britain, the Empire and America alone. Eventually it would sell many more. It was translated into virtually every European language. The tiger skin that the lovers reclined on became a favourite cliché of the age.*

Elinor toured the world, coasting the wave of fame. Just before her forty-third birthday, she set sail for America, with 60 pairs of high-heeled shoes neatly packed. The New York press loved her, and she took tea with a literary giant, the elderly and white-haired Mark Twain. She then toured the Wild West, and on her visit to Rawhide, Nevada, she was serenaded by hundreds of gold miners. She was impressed by 'nature's gentlemen' and for the first time moved beyond the straitjacket of her Victorian upbringing, realising that true gentility was not dependent on social rank. Yet the surge of fame was already turning her head. Elinor was falling increasingly under the spell of esoteric philosophy, believing she could conjure up waterfalls of wealth purely by the power of intention.

Her escapades continued to provide fertile material for her novels. One expedition took her deep into the heart of Imperial Russia, into the feverish, decadent banquets that the nobles enjoyed in their magnificent palaces. Her hosts cautioned her to avert her eyes as starving peasants wandered past barefoot in the snow. Elinor cavorted in golden troikas through snowstorms, and toured the Winter Palace, where she solemnly declared herself to be the reincarnation of Catherine the Great.

Yet behind the glorious illusion, things were falling apart. Her husband was dying, his purse empty and his liver shredded. She was forced to concoct a mediocre novel in eighteen days just to stave off his creditors. Her own great and passionate infidelity, with Lord Curzon, the former Viceroy of India, limped on without commitment or resolution. She only learned her ten-year love affair was over when she read in The Times *that he was engaged to another woman. It was a nasty blow for the self-styled queen of romance.*

Elinor escaped to Paris, scoffing lobster, raspberries and cream every day at the Ritz. Then came another terrible, sudden shock. German armies were on the march. In August 1914, Europe tumbled into the abyss, and romantic love was shredded to death on the barbed wire of the Somme. In the poignant words of Larkin, 'Never such innocence again'.

*   *   *

The war proved another fruitful canvas for Elinor; she raced to report from the front line and did menial voluntary work in London. Yet as the dust settled across a scarred and bloodied Europe, what did the future hold? Where could an ageing Romantic, approaching her sixtieth birthday, turn? The answer was simple: to go West.

The Hollywood Hotel
Los Angeles, California
1925

We are present at the creation. In California in the beginning, there must have been an Edenic paradise, of orange groves and eternal sunshine. This was a world of old Spanish missions, of burning heat on adobe walls. Time moved slowly here, unfolding languidly on the sundials, until one day, it started to accelerate into the future.

First men came west for God, then for gold. Now a new breed of technical pioneers has colonised the Promised Land, in search of the aura of pure clear light. Dusty farms have become studios. The merciless Californian sun is the ideal medium for these magicians, as they conjure up ghosts on their magic lanterns. We came here to consult with these wizards of the coast. We checked into an obscure and somewhat ramshackle country roadhouse, the Hollywood Hotel, which has suddenly become deluged with celebrities. The landlady is now a good friend of mine.

Jesse Lasky, the studio supremo, had invited us over. Those early motion pictures were marvellous, but their style was raw and untutored. So, Jesse summoned a brace of established writers, to travel over from old Europe and embrace the uncharted horizons of Hollywood. Most of us failed to grasp the fluid new visual medium of the cinema; and were soon sent packing. Even the great Somerset Maugham lasted only a week here. I took to it like a duck to water.

California is the ultimate reversal. Sunlight is burning away the cloying Jersey fog of my past, scourging and renewing me from within. In England they dismissed me as a mere scribbler, a purveyor of pot-boilers; over here the sheer popularity of my books is validation enough. In Jersey as a child, they pitied and scorned my unconventional looks; remember that threat of the leaden comb, and all those whispered asides? Here, they adore me. Gloria Swanson loves my striking red hair and my theatrical poise; I receive daily compliments about my piercing green eyes.

There is a new world here, and it is in the process of being born. They are busy ploughing boulevards, excavating great highways across empty scrubland and new roads along twisting canyons. They are planting young palm trees outside, in neat rows along the boulevards. Beverly Hills often seems like a dusty building site, with estates of grand houses springing up overnight like mushrooms. The sidewalks vanish into empty fields, but we know those fields will soon be filled. We perch here above a thousand miles of azure ocean, where the brown hills dissolve into pure clear light. This is where the great trek west ended, where the restless American frontier reached its final destination. I am living in this promised land.

My first major cinematic breakthrough was *Beyond the Rocks*, which starred

Gloria Swanson and Rudolph Valentino. Now I glide through the opulent salons of William Randolph Hearst. I waltz at parties with Douglas Fairbanks and Mary Pickford, the golden couple of the silent movies. It is as if I am a house guest at a beautiful and shining ball.

Weekends are spent unwinding and playing charades with Charles Chaplin. He is such a riot! Can you believe this is the lost boy whose hair was doused in iodine in the Hanwell workhouse? He was an unknown theatre clown, when he was captured on film for the first time in my beautiful home Island of Jersey. Now, by a dazzling series of miracles, this wonderful human being has ended up as the most famous man in the world.

We've had such tremendous fun together, and one fine morning we even eloped down to Mexico! He'd just married young Lita Grey, and after a madcap road trip, we all ended up in a decrepit double-bedded shack in a tiny Mexican village! Charles and Lita shared a bed while I curled up in a makeshift cot in the corner. We were just drifting off to sleep when Charles, with impeccable comic timing, intoned in a sepulchral voice: "My God! Think of Charlie Chaplin and Elinor Glyn in bed together in the wilds of Mexico". He then ad-libbed some hilarious press reports of the incident!

It is a beautiful life; a fairy tale as poetic as any of the endings to my novels. I wake every morning, and the blazing sun warms my bones. My past in Jersey and England has receded to the form of a distant, troubling dream. The longer I am here, the further away I feel. It is a blissful thought. Yet somehow, far beneath the waterline, I sense that my soul is already beginning to fray.

*　*　*

Early Hollywood left an indelible mark on those in its orbit, far deeper than the noxious mercury vapours from the Cooper-Hewitt lamps that stained even Elinor's red hair a violent purple. The allure of the West Coast sucked in a swarm of writers and swindlers, moneymen and showgirls, tycoons on the make, hunters and their prey. This was a gold rush as fatal and alluring as the mad old days of 1849; the spell of California promising untold wealth to the ferociously ambitious with nothing to lose but their souls.

The paranoia and fearful undercurrents of Hollywood gradually corroded Elinor's frail peace of mind. Gradually Elinor Glyn, ever attuned to the esoteric, believed that the entire West Coast was caught in the grip of an ancient curse. The first symptoms she noted, that became immediately evident upon arrival in Hollywood, were a 'sense of exaggerated self-importance and self-centredness'. The next stage, to which she pleaded guilty, was a sudden and consuming obsession with making money. She herself realised she had become infected with the virus. The final and fatal stage, Elinor argued, was utter moral bankruptcy.

Hollywood indeed consumed so many of its children. Morphine, moonshine and mistresses flourished in the hothouse atmosphere of the West Coast. Was Elinor simply blinded by the Klieg lights, those dazzling studio arc lamps that burned the eyes of many a star? Elinor already suspected she had drunk a little too deeply of the mad, befuddling wine of Hollywood, long before she ever set sail on a yacht called the Oneida, *on a tragic voyage that would enter into the legends of Hollywood noir.*

Yet in 1927 she had one magical swansong to bestow, the movie 'It'. Starring the irrepressible Clara Bow, this movie was Elinor Glyn's masterpiece. The concept of the 'It Girl' – someone blessed with innate, effortless charisma and magnetism – has since become part of the English language.

Bow was an inspired piece of casting; a devastatingly appealing young woman who seemed utterly modern in her self-reliance and sheer verve. The movie's sassy star helped 'It' make a million dollars in profit, and sealed Elinor's reputation in Hollywood. The 'It Girl', as much as the Charleston dance or the Flapper, became a cultural phenomenon and sign of the times.

'It' had always been the animating spirit of all of Elinor's romances, a poetic short hand for a magnetic allure and beguiling appeal that transcended the purely physical. The Roaring Twenties were made for the 'It Girls'. This was the Jazz Age, an era of effortless style, easy money and easier morals, and Elinor Glyn captured its heart.

Yet by now Elinor herself was playing another role, of victim. It was famously said that she was never offered a contract she wouldn't sign. She foolishly allowed herself to be seduced by a succession of charming and financially manipulative young men. Bleeding money, she retreated from the West Coast.

She attempted to recreate her magic in England; but far from the technical mastery of Hollywood, her motion pictures proved dismal failures. Virtually bankrupt and alone, she was compelled to write her engaging and intimate autobiography, Romantic Adventure, *to stave off the renewed threat of destitution. Her beautiful dream was over.*

In the end, there was just one more pilgrimage Elinor Glyn could make. In February 1939, this elderly woman returned to Jersey, the Island of her birth, for the first time in over fifty long years. It was a triumphant homecoming. Great parties were held in her honour; the Bailiff presented her with the Great Seal of the Island. Elinor toured her old haunts; privately cherishing the glimpse of the parapet where she had once shared her first kiss with an Eton boy.

The Jersey Evening Post, *on 10th February 1939, prominently reported the talk that Elinor Glyn delivered to the Rotary Club in the Halkett Hotel next to Royal Square. She charmed the audience with her childhood memories of the Island. She fondly recalled falling asleep on the footstall as a little child during tedious sermons at St Mark's Church. She explained how strangely familiar it felt, to climb the staircase at Government House. Fifty years had merely been the blink of an eye. That was the place where she sneaked under a table with her sister and a friend to catch a glimpse of the impossibly glamorous Lillie Langtry. A giggle gave them away; but the divine Mrs Langtry promised to say nothing, and even ordered some supper for the little girls. Elinor's homecoming speech ended in hearty applause.*

Elinor's public stance was one of pride and gratitude to the Island of her birth. Privately, she found the return visit profoundly disturbing. She felt standards had slipped; Government House seemed a shadow of its former eminence. The Jersey of her childhood had grown cramped and small, full, she wrote of 'bad, petty and envious vibrations'. St Helier now seemed a cramped and diminished place compared to the exhilarating space and seductive vistas of California. The curse of the West Coast had left an indelible mark.

Elinor searched in vain for the house where she was born, but it had long gone. Everything had changed for the worse; her childhood world had irredeemably fled. She appreciated the flowers and kindness from her native Island, but in the end parted with a sad and tormented farewell. She wrote privately: 'I remember now feeling on the boat in 1888 when we finally left, the prison doors were opening at last.... I never wish to go back again'.

She never did. As Nazi bombs pummelled London and her birthplace fell into the shadow of the Occupation, Elinor Glyn gradually slipped away. Some of her very last letters were to William Randolph Hearst and Marion Davies, sent from battered, blacked-out London and winging far away to their glittering Californian palace at San Simeon. Elinor fell into the shadow of her own memories.

*   *   *

Elinor Glyn
London, September 1942

'We live as we dream, alone'. Every night the black mountain-tides of Jersey are raging in my nightmares, flooding towards me, and seeking to drag me under. I am gasping for breath, fighting for life, so I wake. Even as the night terrors fade, I listen to the deadly symphony of the small hours; the spine-tingling wail of the air raid sirens and the dull thud of the German bombs.

The sky is on fire here every night. I am almost bed-ridden, bent double in a silken prison. Still, I often press my face to the window and spy the curtains of flame sweeping westward across the heart of the city. London is a like a bloodied boxer, slugged hard to the ground, losing a tooth or an eye, but fighting back with fury against the darkness. I am so proud. I shall not yield either, so my gas mask remains neatly boxed under the dressing table. I simply lie on my bed, listening to the murderous thunder, waiting to see if I will suddenly burn.

At first, they wanted to evacuate me to the country, and while the raids were at their fiercest, I did retreat to my old house at Miskin Manor. Yet I could not stay, for every room was shrieking with memories. I could no longer face the deathly corridor where my mother once paced like a wizened ghost, a pale old lady with cap and cane who would not let me be. I cannot escape her, though, for in these latter days, I have become her. The royal romances, the tiger skins and seductive vistas of Hollywood have all led here, to this lonely room full of memories.

They say lately that the news is better; the fortunes of war are turning. The radio tells of vast, hellish battles, of thousands of tanks colliding and clashing on the great Russian plains. I drift away through the unruly continents of my own mind. I remember those great ice-draped palaces of Moscow, the golden troikas gliding like swans across the snowfields. I remember the feasts, the fabulous balls, the revels of the old regime. Those palaces burned long ago, under a red star. My hosts were shot at dawn.

I sometimes feel that all the beauty in the world has fled. At the height of my fame, I travelled to Rawhide, Nevada, to dine with the goldminers, the finest nobles of the earth. It was one of the proudest moments of my life as I held court with those decent, honest men. One of those gallant gentlemen even rode ninety miles across the desert, just to present me with a bunch of yellow daisies. Today that gold-rush town has been swallowed up by the earth, the empty schools and hotels looming in the swirling dust. I recall the eerie lines from Shelley I read so long ago in the library at Richelieu in Jersey: 'Nothing beside remains'.

The California Curse has devoured me from within. For a fleeting, capricious moment, I stood at the pinnacle of Hollywood, as Clara Bow wowed the world and my films grossed a million dollars apiece. For a time, I even believed I could simply speak riches into the world as if by a golden spell. Now silent films are history, an embarrassment. All my wealth has seeped away like water, like dear old Clayton's before me, flowing back to the silent places of the earth.

This is how it was always going to end. I think of Lucy, my beautiful, late sister. I think of her standing on the gangway to the *Titanic*, blissfully unaware of what was to come, never knowing the voyage that lay ahead. I will be joining her soon on her final journey.

I am weary of it all now, locked in this gilded cage, too exhausted to reveal my face in the world again. The detritus of my life is scattered all around me, in golden caskets crammed with memories. The silk canopy of my bed, the silver-heart shaped mirror on my dressing table; these are trinkets and jewels from a half-forgotten world. I sent a last letter to Marion Davies in Hollywood yesterday, and my shaking hands could barely grasp the pencil to shape each letter. After so long, even my words are being stolen from me.

No matter, for all my stories are told. All the weddings are done, the confetti spilt, and the heroes are living happily ever after, or lying in coffins from the wars. I hear all their voices crowding in my dreams, a cacophony of beauty and life, like radio broadcasts from a distant star. The tiger skin is packed away, forgotten, waiting for another age. Romance is my lodestar, but now the dream is done.

Far above my silken shroud, the searchlights scour the sky, bringing false dawn, reminding me of the distress flares I once saw above a sinking ship, the steamship to Jersey, on a barren rock so long ago. I am confused and befuddled, my spirit broken. I glance for a last time into the silver mirror, in the clear moonlight.

The face of the old, withered woman is gone. Staring back are the red tresses and shining green eyes of a little shipwrecked girl, perched on that rocky ledge, waiting for the waves to come. The waters are lapping at her feet now, the storm tide is roaring in, and soon she will slip away into the night.

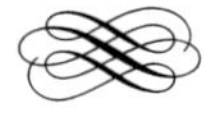

Winter

AGE
OF
WAR

White Star, Blue Iceberg:
The *Titanic* Story

As Elinor's novels sold by the million, her sister Lucy carved out her own dazzling reputation. The fashion empire that she founded on her kitchen table, Lucile Ltd, soon beguiled the world. Her shimmering creations have become the toast of the London and Paris cognoscenti. Some say Lucy enjoys a charmed life.

Spring in New York now beckons, and with it a fresh whirlwind of business engagements. All her decisions, all her struggles, all her triumphs, have somehow led her here; to the delicious decadence of a first-class suite, snugly ensconced in the fastest ship in the world.

It is the shivering night of April 14, 1912, and the maiden voyage of White Star's new flagship is proceeding with the utmost elegance and precision. They say the liner is on course to reach New York in record time. RMS Titanic is about four hundred miles from land now, racing through the icefields, on the brink of its collision with history.

*   *   *

Lady Lucy Duff-Gordon
'A' Deck – RMS *Titanic*
North Atlantic Ocean
April 14, 1912

> *Sing a song of sixpence, a pocket full of rye.*
> *Four and twenty blackbirds baked in a pie.*

My little sister Elinor used to sing those words to me. So, I rattle the old nursery rhyme around my shivering mind, conjuring up the familiar words, willing myself to sink into sleep. But it isn't so easy, for the night is breathing ice. The electric heater in our cabin has rattled away for hours, but it seems to make precious little difference. We are gliding through these silent miles of darkness, so far away from land. But I am restlessly dreaming, of the Jersey of long ago, of the innocence I left behind.

Elinor is calling me, and the years fall from my shoulders like a gown. I am back home again, at No. 55 Colomberie, the street of dovecots; back in the cage of my childhood. Our house rings with quarrels. My livid, tight-fisted, stepfather is reeking of whisky again, and I will not tolerate his rage. So: I slam the door and retreat to the upper room, my precious sanctuary. This is the place where one day I stop making clothes for my dolls and start to sew them for my little sister Elinor instead. She takes the pretty gown I have just made for her, and she smiles.

When the pie was opened, the birds began to sing. The years turn. Three love affairs and broken engagements in three dizzy months; three hearts left broken. I waltz once more through that reckless summer when I fall in love with a dashing Jersey captain, and then feud with him, casting aside my pearl beyond price. I wince at the day that I storm away from him, and never come home to Jersey again.

I dance through the rest of my life's story, of my impetuous marriage to a wine-drenched cheat, the happy birth of my daughter; the grinding money-mill of the London divorce courts. Then I am carving out my own future, through the fashion business I found on my kitchen table. I call it Maison Lucile: it becomes a whirlwind of tea-gowns, of shimmering diaphanous dresses and eye-catching mannequin parades. I remarry, and my success grows. Through my bold and flirtatious designs, I conjure up a waterfall of wealth, of Paris shows and grand American expansion plans. *Wasn't that a dainty dish, to set before the king?*

Then there's the urgent business that calls me to New York; the clerk at the White Star booking office who only beams at me when I draw back, when I feel a strange and most peculiar moment of hesitation. Only the brand-new RMS *Titanic* has tickets available at such short notice. A fabulous maiden voyage, on the largest liner in the world. "This ship will make history!", the clerk smiles.

And indeed, it has, with all the plump fresh strawberries they whisk up for me at breakfast, the spectacular baroque decks, the warmth and luxury of an English country house, gliding through the vast and freezing ocean. Yet that first stubborn shiver will not leave me. "I have never felt so cold", I confide to my husband Cosmo as we descend to the restaurant. "There must be icebergs around".

The king is in the counting-house, counting out his money. Dinner last night was sumptuous, although I opted to dine in my furs because of the icy chill. The A La Carte restaurant is a delightful fantasia, carved out of French walnut and softened by thick Axminster carpet. Bruce Ismay, chairman of the White Star Line, is holding court at the next table. Laughter floats from across the room, where white-bearded Captain Smith is entertaining a fat ledger of American multi-millionaires. He always has such a charming way with the guests; perhaps he is more impresario than seaman. He will doubtless enjoy his well-earned retirement after this journey is done.

Further across the lavish salon, old Colonel Astor gazes deeply and longingly into the eyes of his stunning eighteen-year-old bride. Winter has married Spring after all. She looks vaguely bored by the feast. But they do say he is one of the richest men in the world.

The queen was in the parlour, eating bread and honey. The cuisine here is exceptional; oysters and filet mignon; Waldorf pudding and peaches smothered in Chartreuse jelly. Fresh daffodils bloom riotously on our dinner table, as if they have been plucked fresh from a Jersey hillside! We are in the hands of the sublime London restaurateur Gatti, and his creations are a tantalising delight. Why, you would think you were at the Ritz! Laughter floats across the room, as wealthy gentlemen lay lavish bets on our arrival time in New York. RMS *Titanic* is going to beat the Atlantic record; that much is certain. The ship ploughs on into the night.

We drift down to the decadent luxury of the lounge, where we meet Edgar and Leila Meyer. Alas her father, the owner of Saks Fifth Avenue, has just passed away, and so they have had to urgently take the ship home for the funeral. Time to trade autographs and fill in our 'Confession' books, which are all the rage these days. Mr Meyer completes his likes, his abominations and all the rest, and pauses a moment when he comes to the column marked 'madnesses'. He laughs and says: "I have only one: to live!" And we all chortle away together.

The maid was in the garden, hanging out the clothes. I'm back in our cabin now, chatting away by the stove with Miss Francatelli, my personal secretary, as I undress. 'Franks' is as diligent and efficient as ever, and my schedule for arrival in New York is looking pleasantly full. Engagements, meetings, endless press appearances; the stuff that money is made of. And so, to bed.

Lights out now, drifting away with the comforting hum of the engines, deep into the night. I idly remember the £50,000 necklace stowed in my cabin, and how gorgeous it will look on those Lucile models for the American mannequin parades. It is a long way from the high-ceilinged room at Colomberie where I made my first dresses. I have flown so far and so high, into the thinning, freezing air.

When down came a blackbird. A shadow falls. I hear a giant throwing bowling balls, rumbling and scraping them along the ground. I jolt awake with a start, drunk with sleep, stumbling in a torpor. Something has changed. It takes me a second to realise exactly what has happened.

A bird is falling. The gentle whistle of its song grows into the violent hiss of steam releasing under intense pressure. Something is wrong. The *Titanic*'s engines have stopped.

*   *   *

Alfred Olliver, Quartermaster
Bridge of RMS *Titanic*
April 14, 1912

They say Jerseymen are born to set to sea, and I ran into its embrace when I was only sixteen. I'm a *gris ventre*, a St Ouënnais by birth, the third child of eleven. Only eight of us lived. My father was a Breton farmer; my mother a proud Le Cornu. Her forefathers have dwelled up at Les Landes forever, in the shadow of the ruined castle. They lived where Jersey's grey snout punches into the ocean. That's my home.

They had too many mouths to feed, and there were no prospects at home. So, I took the Queen's shilling and enlisted in the Navy, in the last year of Victoria's reign. They ground me through the hard mill of the Royal Marines training barracks in Gosport. Those were long and gruelling years, but I learned well enough to navigate, to steer and sail. Seawater entered my blood. I served the King for seven years, but with no wars left to fight in this peaceable age, and a wife to win, I eventually decided to slip into a more comfortable berth.

So I joined White Star Line, the king of the ocean passenger firms, ferrying millionaires and commoners alike from the Old World to the New. I was posted to their flagship, RMS *Olympic*, as soon as it came down from the yards at Belfast. That ship, as the press remember too well, courted disaster, scraping poor HMS *Hawke* in the Solent, but despite the Board of Inquiry, I don't blame Captain Smith for that collision. The old man will retire after this voyage with all the credit he deserves.

My new wife and I nestled in the suburbs of Southampton, not far from the dockyards. We named our little home 'Olympic' in honour of the ship, and last year my son was born. Rents being as expensive as they are, we share the house with my brother-in-law Walter, who also works on the ships. That's how we both came to be transferred to RMS *Titanic*, newest of the lot. The maiden voyage of a new White Star liner is always something special, and I am looking forward to docking on Manhattan Island come the seventeenth. New York is quite a city.

This evening my duties have included helming the ship, with my hands grasping the wheel as it plunges through the North Atlantic. This ship surely lives up to its name. It is the largest man-made object in the world. As I steer, I think of the 882 feet of steel, the three million rivets, the twenty-nine boilers driving the great vessel forwards. We travel at a brisk 22 knots, ploughing through the Atlantic miles like a knife through butter.

They say the richest man in Babylon is aboard tonight, John Jacob Astor himself, and perhaps one of the noblest too, the earnest reformer William Stead, on his way to a peace conference. The boss himself, Bruce Ismay, chairman of the line, is on board, so we are all on our sharpest behaviour. Capt. Smith is doubtless wining and dining the First-class passengers right now; rank has its privileges. Let them all enjoy the swimming pool, the Turkish baths and squash courts. I am here to work.

At ten o'clock, I am finally relieved of the wheel. The dog hours of the later watches are proving to be the usual flurry of errands and tasks, for a Quartermaster's work is never done. I have just been trimming the lights in the standing compass, so they would burn properly. Then three sharp bells ring out from the Crow's Nest. Fred Fleet must have seen something. I can only see the blackness of the night.

I step onto the bridge. The ship is veering drunkenly to port. Then there is a prolonged shudder, like a rolling earthquake, and a long, grinding sound, as if cutting the top off a tin can.

The bridge is in darkness, which is standard procedure on the night watch. My eyes take a moment to adjust. William Murdoch, officer of the watch, is at the engine order telegraph. Over in the wheelhouse, I can make out Mr Moody's silhouette, and Robert Hichens grasping the wheel, frozen like a waxwork. Thank God, this fiasco didn't happen on my watch. There will be hell to pay if the ship has hit something. Perhaps our pay will be docked.

Then I see the jagged alp of ice. It is sweeping right past the bridge. It's a little higher than the deck, with a brutal spiked crown. I have never seen an iceberg so close, and it looks so dark-blue, so heavy, as if it's filled right up with the ocean. I shudder at the evil sight, but it falls away astern, back into the night.

"Hard a-port", Murdoch cries. The vicious grinding stops. He's already signalled to shut down the engines. Now he turns the lever to shut the watertight doors. Then Captain Smith, who has been resting, stumbles onto the bridge: "Mr Murdoch, what was that?"

"An iceberg, sir."

"Close the watertight doors," the Captain orders.

"The watertight doors are closed, sir."

I glance over at the clock at the back of the wheelhouse. It is twenty minutes to midnight. There is a sudden, almost deafening, silence, for the heartbeat of my working life has suddenly fallen still. The *Titanic*'s engines have stopped.

*　　*　　*

The fatal wound proves to be a slender touch, barely an inch high. Yet it has slashed a vicious two hundred-and-fifty-foot tear across the starboard hull of the ship. From the moment that the fifth watertight compartment was breached, the fate of RMS Titanic was sealed. The iron laws of physics would brook no argument. The fatal plunge, over two miles down to oblivion, is now only a matter of time.

Yet in these strange, suspended hours, it almost feels as if nothing has changed, as the Captain puts the ship into 'slow ahead' and the crew frantically scramble to assess the extent of the damage. Guests turn over and drift back to their inebriated, comfortable sleep. A few passengers kick around the wedges of ice on the deck; some enjoy the novelty of fresh ice in their whisky. In their minds, the safe berth in New York is still drawing them all home.

Gravity has different plans. Lucy's fifty-thousand-pound necklace, the brace of gleaming new Renault cars, the nurseries stuffed with children's toys; the sumptuous Turkish baths; the lavishly equipped gymnasium; the hot and crowded third-class decks, the astonishingly elegant French restaurant; the great wheelhouse; the vases blooming with the fresh daffodils of Spring; cargoes of orchids, champagne and golf balls; sacks of undelivered mail; the cutting-edge Marconi wireless machines; the gruel and slop vats in the third-class kitchens. In two hours and forty minutes, all of this will be cast down into the abyss, plunging down to the black sea-bed of the North Atlantic.

The water is already flooding in fast through the breach, flooding the furnaces and drowning the third-class cabins closest to the bow. Millionaires with thousands of dollars stuffed in their pockets; impoverished migrant labourers with little but the clothes on their back: the icy ocean would come for them all.

The ship's final roster at Queenstown reported 3,327 passengers and crew on board; the lifeboats could carry a maximum of 1,178 people. As the strange rumbling sound came to an end, and the passengers drifted back into their sleep, simple mathematics dictated that almost two-thirds of them were already dead. The eventual toll would prove to be much higher.

Yet Lady Lucy Duff-Gordon only hears a euphoric, boyish cry of amazement from somewhere outside as she awakes in her pretty pink cabin. "Ha! There's ice on the deck!", someone cries. We must have scraped a 'berg". The sound of hooting, boisterous laughter spills into her cabin.

Lady Lucy Duff-Gordon
'A' Deck – First Class cabin, RMS *Titanic*
April 14, 1912

Time to wake Cosmo. I tiptoe over to his separate cabin. It is fair to say that our marriage has long since spent its passion and has meandered into the by-waters of convenience. Typically, Cosmo is livid at the interruption to his sleep and only too happy to hold forth with injured bluster: "Don't be ridiculous, Lucy. Even if it was an iceberg, it can't do any serious damage. The ship is built on a series of interlocking watertight compartments. It is designed expressly not to sink!" His hitherto unknown talents in the field of marine engineering are scarcely reassuring.

I am not taking his dull complacency for an answer. I badger and goad Cosmo into dressing, and like a huffing and shuffling old bear, he eventually puts on his clothes and ambles up to the deck. As the door opens, I hear him passing a steward in the corridor, as cloying and obsequious as ever. "There is nothing to worry about sir. Please return to your cabin". He brushes the flunkey aside and blunders on up to the First-class salon, determined as usual to prove his wife wrong.

I lie here alone, nestled in the soft pink bosom of my cabin. It is so cosy, so comforting, with the array of photographs and lace quilts. I could be in a hotel bedroom on land, somewhere in the heart of the Jersey countryside. I love the telephone, the piping hot water, even the fancy soft lights that automatically turn on when I step into the shower. Perhaps my doubts are unfounded after all, and my fearful imagination is running away with me. I am nestled in the largest moving object on the face of the Earth, after all. Yet I can sense that the solid floor beneath my feet is beginning, almost imperceptibly, to tilt.

Cosmo strides back in. Even before he speaks, I recognise the tightness in his jaw; it is rising and barely suppressed fear. He tersely informs me that he has bumped into John Jacob Astor, the richest and most well-connected man on God's earth. The situation is far graver than anyone is letting on. Jack has already advised his wife to put on warm clothes and prepare for the lifeboats. Like a startled rabbit, I rush to the wardrobe and gather my warmest furs, and my greatest coat.

A knock at the door. Miss Francatelli, usually a bastion of unflappable poise, bursts in, in a state of near-hysterics. She has come up from her cabin four floors down, on E-deck. Seawater is rising quickly up the corridors, and her own cabin is flooding. She hears rumours that they are already uncovering the lifeboats on the deck. She is certain of it: the ship is going down.

A second knock at the door. Another strained, ingratiating smile from the very steward who only minutes before had been telling passengers not to worry. "Sorry to disturb you ma'am, but the Captain's orders are to put on lifebelts."

Surprisingly, despite all I have heard, I feel a sudden pang of irritation. What officious, fussy madness to make us leave the bosom of our cabin, don a ridiculous life-preserver and muster on deck in the cold of the night! I look around, for a final time, at my gorgeous pink boudoir. The ice-white lilies of the valley, a parting gift from the Lucile girls in Paris, smile back at me. This pretty, gorgeous little sanctuary begs me to wait a while, to linger in its soft embrace. As I leave, a vase of fresh flowers slides off the washstand, and shatters into pieces on the floor.

*　*　*

Alfred Olliver, Quartermaster
Bridge of RMS *Titanic*
April 14, 1912

Captain Smith wrote out the note itself, folded it neatly and entrusted it to my hands, to deliver it in person to the Chief Engineer. I wouldn't dream of breaking his confidence and reading it – that would be an unpardonable breach. I might even get dismissed on the spot, and who would look after Amelia and the baby then? And part of me, too, was dreading exactly what might have been written.

I clattered down the gangways, and along Scotland Road as we call it, deep into the bowels of the ship. It was still hot down there, even though the engines were stilled. I reached the engine room, and it was the very heart of darkness, blacker than midwinter at Grosnez when I was a lad. The lights were flickering and going out one by one down there, like stars on a cloudy night.

I saw shadows emerging from the stokehold, the grimy stokers stepping aside from their work. But their furnaces were black. Then I made out the silhouette of the Chief Engineer and passed him a note. I saw his men gingerly open the watertight doors that had crashed down after the collision. A brave man stepped into the darkened stokehold to assess the damage. Minutes passed.

Then the investigation was done. The Chief Engineer turned to me, and his eyes were gleaming in the heat and darkness. He spoke tersely, as if the pressure would break him. "Tell the Captain: I will get it done as soon as possible. I will get it done as soon as possible." As I climbed up into the light to deliver his message, I felt as if I had crawled alive out of the catacombs.

I hurried up to the bridge. The ship seemed calm, frozen in the sluggish aftermath of the impact. Then I delivered the words I was meant to convey. Captain Smith nodded, and he was looking strange at me and afar, as if he had spotted something on the horizon. Then he sent me off to the boatswain, with an instruction to get the oar lines and uncover the boats. I have lived long enough at sea to know what he meant. It was time to abandon ship.

*   *   *

As RMS Titanic's *bow slouches ever lower, the floodwaters begin to rise. They drown the orlop deck first, sweeping up through the mail room, drowning the sacks of love letters, the share certificates, the tax demands; all the mundane correspondence of transatlantic trade. The icy ocean floods into burning-hot boiler rooms, sending choking clouds of steam belching out of its funnels. In the Marconi room, the operators remain on duty, sending desperate cries for help into the void. The* Carpathia, *sixty miles to the south, hears the cries and makes immediate haste for the rescue. It will arrive too late. Like a great and wounded whale, the Titanic is already dying.*

The exquisitely calibrated social order of pre-war England is gradually collapsing. In the chaos, messages become confused and arbitrary; on the starboard side, the order of evacuation is women and children first; on the port side, the policy is strictly interpreted as women and children only. Alfred Olliver reports for duty at his assigned boat, Lifeboat Number 5. Bruce Ismay, millionaire chairman of the White Star line, is supervising proceedings, demanding faster progress, ordering Lifeboat 5 to be lowered at once. Officer Rowe, angered by this interfering know-it-all, angrily swears directly to his face. This astonishing breach of etiquette slips by unheeded; a new order of things has begun.

Lifeboat 5 is crawling like a snail down the side of the ship. Yet it is lurching violently on its davits, half poised to scatter its passengers into the brine. Several heavy men leap down into the boat, desperate to save themselves, and the impact causes the boat to swivel alarmingly. Alfred Olliver realises there is another, greater, danger: the plugholes in the boat are lying wide open. Unless he can immediately put the stoppers in, the passengers will simply have exchanged one sinking ship for a smaller one. Yet in the pandemonium, despite his earnest entreaties, no-one will move to make way for him.

More passengers are allowed to board; and eventually the heavily-laden lifeboat strikes the water. Suddenly a surge of ocean water floods in, and there are screams. Alfred forces his way to the bottom of the boat, working like an ox in the freezing darkness, as ice-water pours in. With brute strength, the Jerseyman manages to plug the boat. Lifeboat 5 is saved from utter ruin. There is no moment of respite. The crewmen take straight to the oars and pull as far away from the doomed liner as their strength will take them.

*   *   *

On the Titanic's listing deck, Lucy shivers in the freezing night, despite her furs. The port side of the liner is erupting. Social order is collapsing, as passengers from the lower decks surge forward, threatening to swarm the lifeboats. Lucy shudders at the sight of the desperate mob, and she is sure she must have heard the sharp crack of a revolver. Yet such is the vastness of the Titanic that, while crowds mass in some quarters of the ship, other areas remain eerily quiet. "Let us try the starboard side – it can hardly be as bad there!", her husband Cosmo suggests. Hand in hand, with their secretary Miss Franks in tow, they scramble to the far side of the liner, where First Officer Murdoch is overseeing the lowering of the boats.

Officers try to usher Lucy into one of the regular lifeboats, but she refuses to leave her husband. He is a disappointing man in so many ways; yet why should he be cast aside to his death like a discarded toy? Up front, an emergency cutter is launching, but only a handful of crew members are on it. Cosmo asks politely and gently if his party may board, and he is permitted to do so; refusal would have been absurd given the rows of empty seats.

A gaggle of grimy stokers, refugees from the drowning hell of the engine room, clamber aboard at the last moment, but otherwise the craft is still largely empty as it is lowered slowly down the side of the ship. Lucy curses the cold and longs for the warm embrace of the liner she is leaving behind. Yet the prow is listing alarmingly, and the floodwaters are rising; and just before one o'clock, the Titanic's *engines fall silent for the last time.*

All is not well here on the cutter; one of the lowering ropes is jammed. For a handful of perilous moments, the escapees from First Class are suspended in mid-air, caught between the sinking ship and the freezing ocean below. Like a puppet on strings, a character in the theatre, she twists above the void. First Officer Murdoch calls for a knife, but none is to be found. "Mind your heads!" he cries, and in a surge of anger and frustration, he hurls a heavy bar of metal down against the boat. The sheer force of the impact breaks it free.

The little lifeboat splashes down into the North Atlantic; with only twelve souls aboard, in a craft designed for forty. Lucy is suddenly felled by a violent wave of seasickness. Her dinner bursts out over her gorgeous silk kimono and she is floundering like an eel on the deck of the tub. The lifeboat rows hard into the night. Lucy looks up. Far from land, the sky glows as brightly as a luminous quilt. She gazes up at the white stars, and they seem as remote and indifferent as ice.

Far above, she sees a battery of distress rockets blast into the freezing Atlantic night, their shells showering a constellation of white flares high above the doomed ship. Lucy winces as her ears are deafened for a moment, and her head burns with the echoes. The crack of the explosion booms across the black ocean, like thunder over the horizon, and falls away into the night.

Slumped in the belly of the boat, Lucy feels the silence flood back in. Then she fancies she catches the strains of a jaunty ragtime beat, floating across the darkness. It falls upon the gaggle of boats, from somewhere unseen and half-remembered, like music from a fading star.

*   *   *

In the midst of unspeakable tragedy, comes a strange moment of levity. In Lifeboat No 1, Lucy teases her secretary Miss Francatelli about her shockingly mismatched clothes, which she had thrown on in thirty seconds as the water surged into her cabin. The ladies reminisce longingly about their fabulous, expensive dresses; all of which would shortly be plummeting to the bottom of the North Atlantic. Some of the rougher crew members, unamused by the sight of the wealthy losing their toys, grumble that they had lost all their kit, and yet their pay would be docked from the moment the ship sank. Regulations and all that.

Cosmo, in a fit of magnanimity that would prove to be his life's undoing, then offers each crewman a fiver to buy some new kit. He breaks out a stash of cigars and shares them with the men, to ward off the numbing cold. They shine like dancing pinpricks of light against the utter vastness of the ocean.

Titanic's deck is now a rising alp, with torrents of water flooding down its corridors and pouring out through the side of the ship. Row after row of portholes slip into the ocean's oblivion, even as the ragtime beat still crosses the void, like a strange and distant memory. As the doomed ship's stern reared ever higher, the tune on the deck changed: to the sad strains of Autumn, *she thought, or was it* Nearer, my God, to thee. *It was hard to be sure at this distance.*

The hand on Cosmo's pocket watch slipped into the second hour of the night. All the davits must be empty now, and all the lifeboats had fled. In the wan moonlight, the survivors in the tiny lifeboats could see men scrambling like ants up the violently sloping deck. The boats rowed further away from the stricken liner. She was slowly slipping into the ocean. The final rockets were fired; the last messages scrambled from the Marconi room as the telegraph's power waned. Then the electric lights finally failed, flickered once more, and died for good. RMS Titanic was swallowed by the night.

At the very end, Lucy turned aside. So, she did not see the largest vessel on Earth splinter like matchwood, the funnels crashing into the sea, crushing men alive. She did not behold the terrible whirlpool that dragged millionaires and paupers alike into the maw of the ocean. She only felt the shock waves from the suction that battered the lifeboats and sent her vomiting once again. Huddled on the deck of the cutter, she could only hear the cries that lingered: for help, for God, for their mothers, for mercy. The lifebelts proved highly effective in preventing drowning; so, the passengers flailing in the water were fated to slowly freeze.

And the lifeboats would not turn back to save them. The living and the dead had been fatally divided, and after fifteen minutes or so the last cries of the men in the water finally ceased. Their echoes continued to burn in the mind, long after the last voices were stilled.

It was done. Then the silent ice-breath of the ocean fell over the little gaggle of listeners. The survivors shivered in the open boats, hundreds of miles from shore, and waited for the dawn.

* * *

In time, both the fashion tycoon from St Helier and the quartermaster from St Ouen were hauled up to testify before the United States Senate. Their testimony is immortalised in the Titanic Inquiry, *which ruthlessly exposed the catalogue of human error, arrogance and sheer chance that had doomed the world's greatest and reputedly unsinkable ship.*

The media firestorm began to rage as soon as the first news filtered out. In Jersey, the Evening Post *initially printed reports that all hands had been saved but was soon forced to print corrections as the devastating scale of the tragedy became clearer. The parishes of Jersey were left to mourn their dead.*

The stain on Cosmo's reputation would never be lifted. To the end of his days, he was dogged by unproven allegations that he had bribed the crew of the lifeboat – at the price of the promised five pounds apiece – to whisk them far away from the wreck and not return for survivors. The 'Duff-Gordon' incident became a cause celebre when the British Wreck Commissioners launched their own rival inquiry into the disaster. Anonymous letter writers wrote wicked denunciations of the baronet and his 'Money Boat'; the yellow press had a field day. There was of course no proof to back the rumours; but the court of social opprobrium proved a stern judge.

Lucy remembered the strange sense of unease she had once felt at the moment of the initial booking and resolved to trust her instincts in the future. In 1915, she was offered a berth on RMS Lusitania. She felt an overwhelming surge of nausea and took that as a clear sign to withdraw her booking. Days later, the great liner was torpedoed and sank with the loss of over a thousand lives.

Alfred Olliver, the Jerseyman who had seen the blue iceberg with his own eyes, would also be scarred for life. He duly testified before Senator Burton at the media circus in Washington and remained a loyal employee of the White Star Line. Yet his emotional health had taken a sudden turn for the worse, and at the age of 28, he would never work at sea again.

The Quartermaster of RMS Titanic returned home to Jersey. He died in St Saviour's Parish, some twenty-two years after the shipwreck that had broken him. He was buried in an unmarked grave.

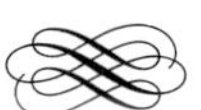

T. B. Davis: The World beyond the Wall

The Titanic *disaster proved a harbinger of the world to come. The ship perfectly captured the well-ordered and deferential society of 1912, from the country-house opulence of the first-class suites to the industrial fires of the boiler room. All of it was headed, fatally and irrevocably, to the bottom of the ocean.*

With hindsight, we can see that the pre-war world was also holed below the waterline, a century of glorious and complacent peace steaming straight towards the slaughterhouse of the Western Front. In the very year the Titanic *set sail, the naval arms race between the Great Powers accelerated, and final preparations for war were being laid. Even in bucolic Jersey, the parish elementary schools had been teaching military drill for well over a decade, in preparation for war.*

There is an appalling clockwork inevitability about the Titanic *disaster that continues to mesmerise. As soon as the fifth watertight compartment was breached, most of the passengers were, mathematically speaking, already dead. Likewise, as soon as the railway timetables were set in motion on the Western Front, the deployment was impossible to revoke. An entire generation had already been doomed.*

There is one Jerseyman above all who embodied the promise and prosperity of the nineteenth century; but who would come to grief in this terrible new world. Tom Davis forged an empire, bound together a continent, and ruled like a king, but in the end, he was unable to save his own.

His story begins long ago, with a ragged boy in a Jersey churchyard.

*   *   *

Tom Davis
St Luke's Church, St Saviour, Jersey
A Sunday morning, 1879

We dreamed of our heist every single moment, as the Sunday service dragged on like a dying dog. The fussy ladies in their hats warbled away like shrivelled old birds, as they always did, and not one of them could sing for toffee. Of course, us boys threw them our best angelic smiles, puffed up in our borrowed choirboy robes, the finest clothes I've ever had the pleasure of wearing. We go to the church school at St Luke's after all, and we have to act the part.

The great church organ booms out like a peal of thunder and the congregation stand up for the liturgy. The offertory plate is coming around now, passed reverently from pew to pew. The congregation cast their silver sixpences and shillings upon the platter and the coins glisten there like a pirate's treasure.

The final hymn is stumbling towards its boisterous end. The organ bellows, crashes and fades away. The Reverend wraps it all up with a mumbled blessing and we dutifully follow him out in the closing procession, parading down the aisle. The pious ladies of St Luke's bow in exaggerated respect as he passes, before they saunter home to their servants, their cooks and their plump well-cushioned libraries.

Well, I'm not going back to my home today, to our soot-black cottage on the Dicq road where I'll shiver on my straw pallet in the upper room. My father, you see, is a fisherman. He works his guts out in high water and rough tides. In winter he's a carpenter in the yards. He reels home every night reeking of tobacco, and spits in front of the fire. He'd have to work a fourteen-hour shift to earn just a couple of the shillings in that collection plate.

At last, our Sunday morning performance is over. "Tom Davis, here are your clothes, boy. Now don't dawdle". The gruff verger hands me my clothes, and they plainly mark out me as a poor boy, as if I had a banner on my forehead. So, I change out of my crimson robes and ruff and swap them back for my torn trousers, my smelly top and my dirty cap. We have to scamper unseen out the back door, so the great and good folk don't have to actually see us urchins.

Then I wink at my best mate Walter, my partner in crime. He knows where we're going next. We've been hatching a plan.

*　　*　　*

There is a tall brick wall that runs right behind St Luke's Church. It has oil lamps along it and red-brown ivy all over it. But it might as well be the Great Wall of China for all we know, for beyond it lies a very different world.

Over that wall lies a grand Jersey estate. Plaisance, they call it. 'Pleasantness', that means, in French. And ruddy pleasant it is too. On my first trespass, I just gawped at it all: the rolling grounds, the manicured bushes, and the great house with its grand bay window and its servants' entrances. They say it even has a dower wing, whatever that means.

My family is holed up at home like rats in our tiny cottage, with hungry babies screaming and more on the way, and this man has a grand hall just for playing billiards. It makes me very curious. What kind of magical powers does he have, to live in a palace like a king? Is he some kind of sorcerer? And if he is, then can I somehow learn his magic?

It's not much of a palace without any guards on the gate. Not so hard for two young lads to clamber up a tree, to shinny up the brickwork, and kick away the shards of broken glass that the groundsman has left up there. We're soon up and over, clean as a whistle. All those cold dawns working on my uncle Winter's fishing boat, have made me as lean as a tomcat. We're soon over the wall. Then we land as gently as ferrets in the orchard, down on those soft and tender lawns.

We're in the closed gardens now, in this world beyond the wall. We're not robbers mind, we both know better than to risk the Constable's anger and end up in borstal for our sins. Our parents would cane us for that. We're trespassing here of course, but we've only come for the chestnuts. Plump and roasted and sweet over the fire, an evening's feast. That's what autumns are made for. And if we only find horse chestnuts, which you can't eat, well we'll just use them for conkers and trade them with the boys at school. The Jurat, the great man that owns this place, doesn't even know we're here. Probably sitting in the smoking room all day, sozzled with all that French wine in his cellar, counting his treasure.

So, we stuff our pockets. It's ridiculously easy, to prise the chestnuts out of their spiny shells. I've got a canvas fisherman's sack with me and we stuff it to the brim. It's a misty autumn morning and the great house beyond is shrouded in a swirl of fog. There are one or two oil lamps burning at the upper windows. Perhaps the servants are making up the beds.

Walter is smirking and we're almost bursting into laughter at the sheer joy of it all. Time to count our pickings, and crawl back to our secret escape route up the brick wall. We're hardly going to just run right out of the main gate, between the great whale-oil lanterns that light the grand entrance to Plaisance.

I lift up Walter and he scrabbles deftly back up the brickwork, using the lead pipework as a foothold. I lob him the bag and he catches it as he climbs. Then, with a final glance into the thickening mist, I place a foot on the stonework and launch myself up.

"Boy – stop right there!" My heart explodes in my ribcage and I feel my blood turn to stone. As if trapped by a spell, I stand with my back against the wall, as if it's going to save me now. Walter plops down by my side. He knows the game is up.

Striding out of the mist towards us, in full morning dress, is a very tall and very angry man. He grabs us both by the scruff of the neck, dragging us away one in each hand, as if we're disobedient dogs.

*　*　*

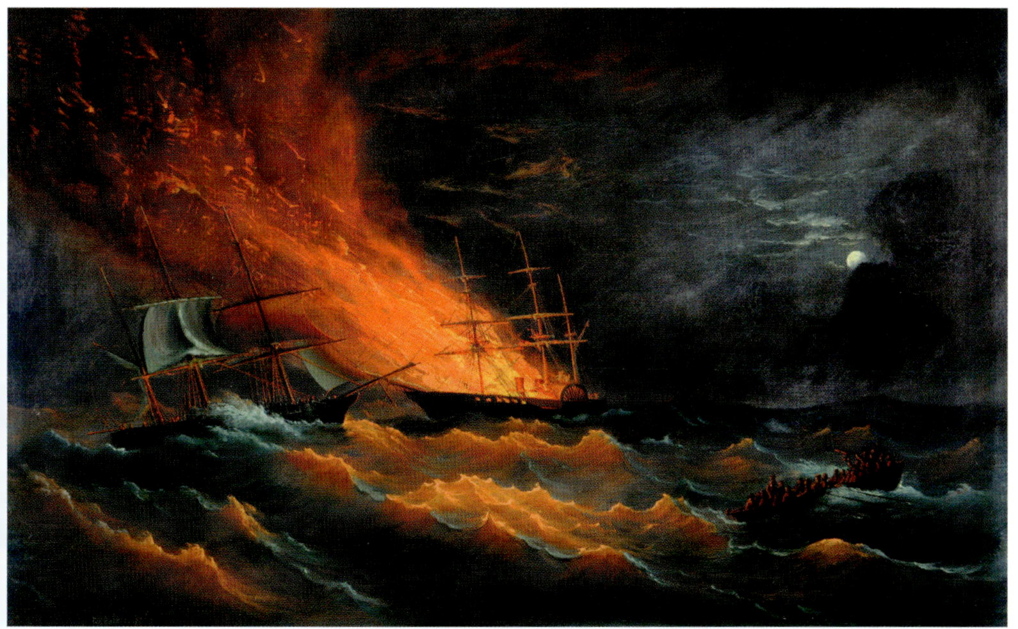

SS Amazon *on Fire in the Bay of Biscay* (1852) by Philip John Ouless (1817-1885)
Courtesy of the Jersey Heritage Collections

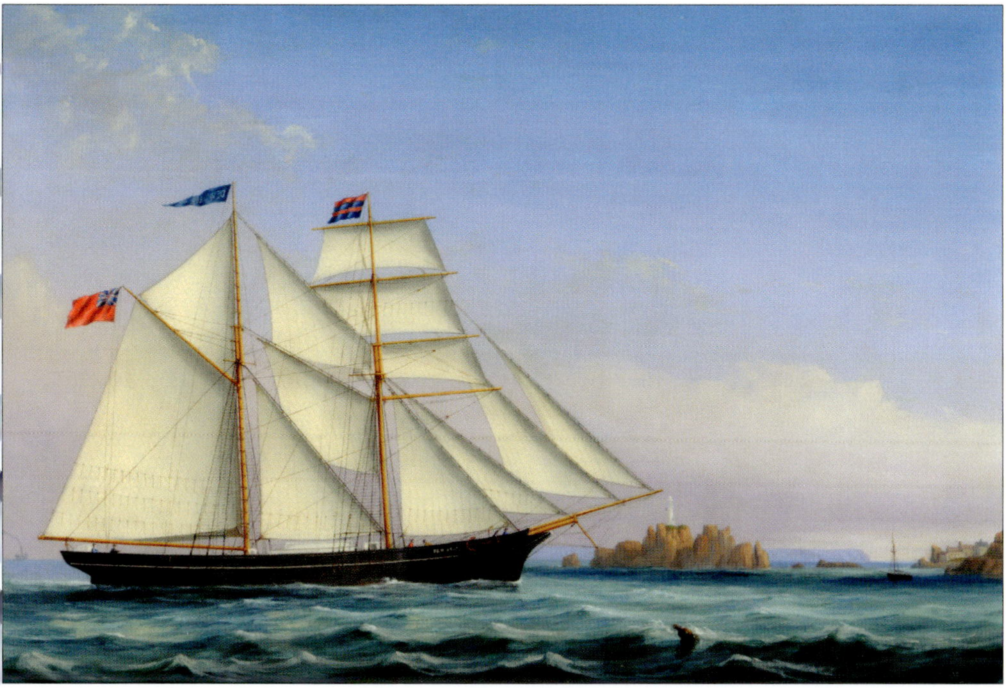

The Dewdrop *off Corbière* (1879) by Philip John Ouless (1817-1885)
Courtesy of the Jersey Heritage Collections

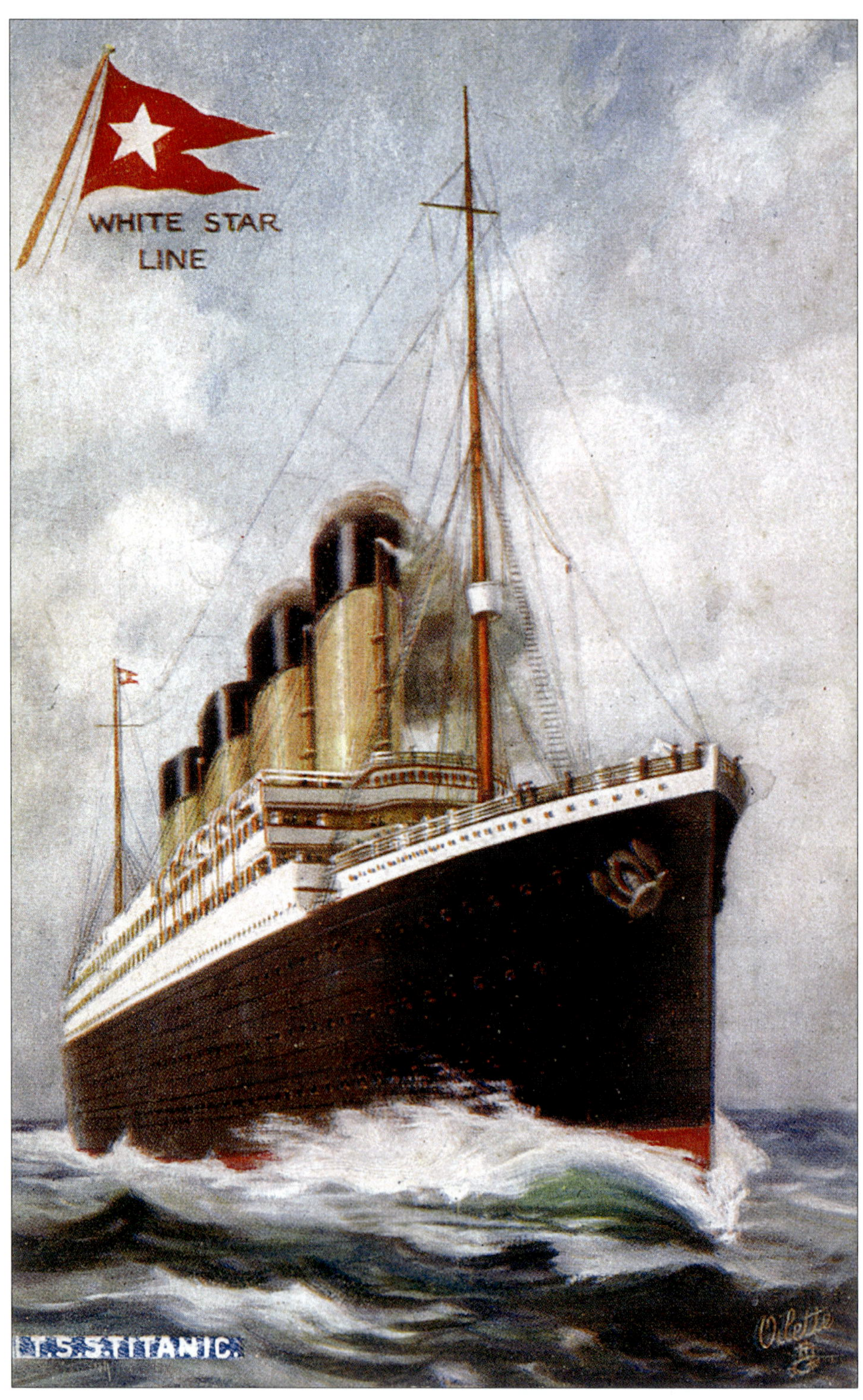

Titanic Postcard (1912)
RMS *Titanic*, passenger liner of the Cunard White Star line
Courtesy of Mary Evans Picture Library

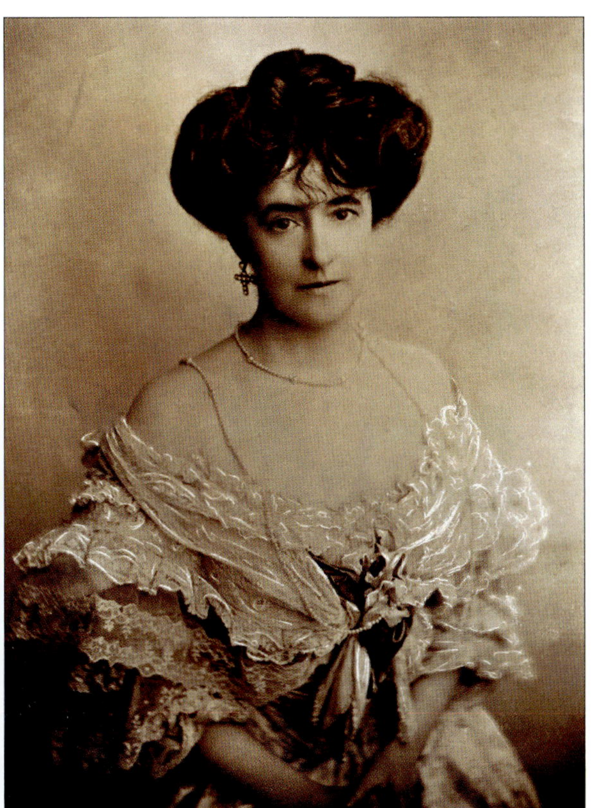

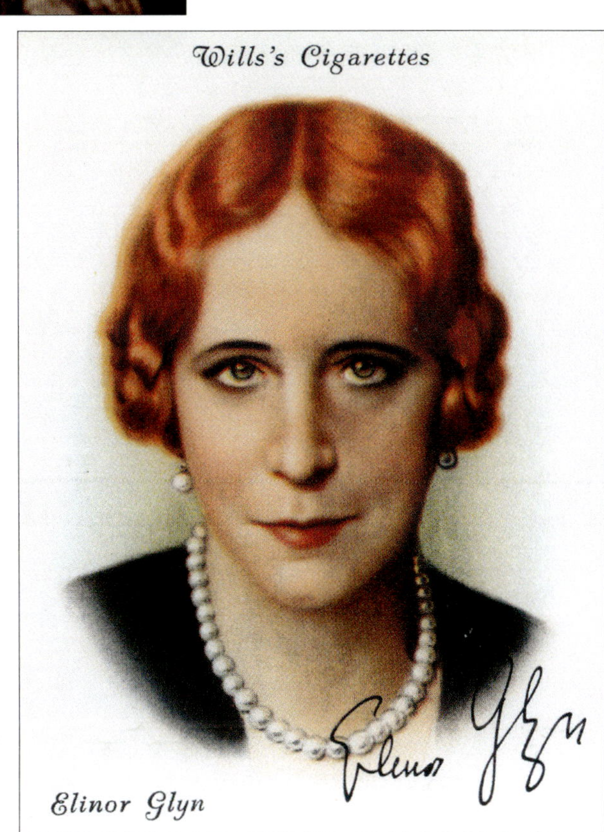

Elinor Glyn after Claude Harris (1937)
© National Portrait Gallery, London

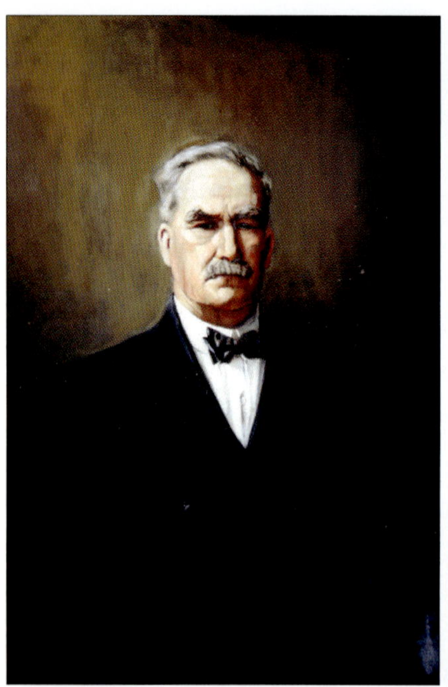

T B Davis by J M Hilson
(b. 1870; date of death unknown)
Courtesy of the Jersey Heritage
Collections

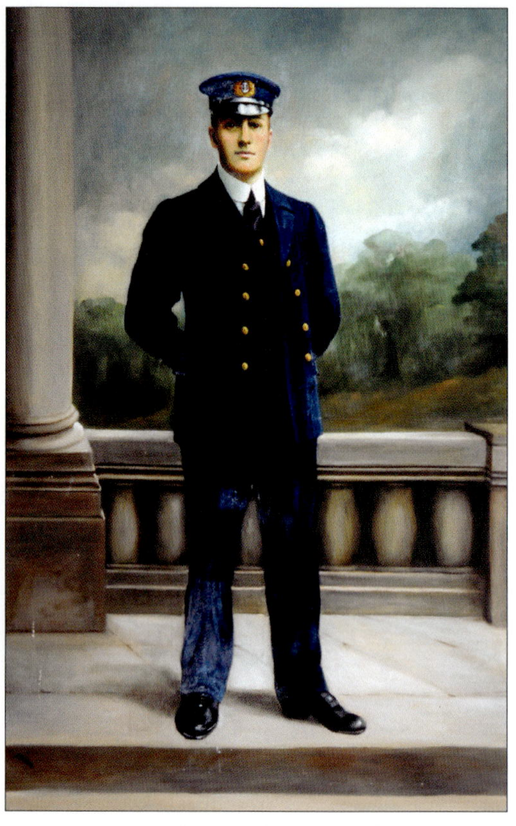

Howard Davis by J M Hilson
(b. 1870; date of death unknown)
Courtesy of the Jersey Heritage Collections

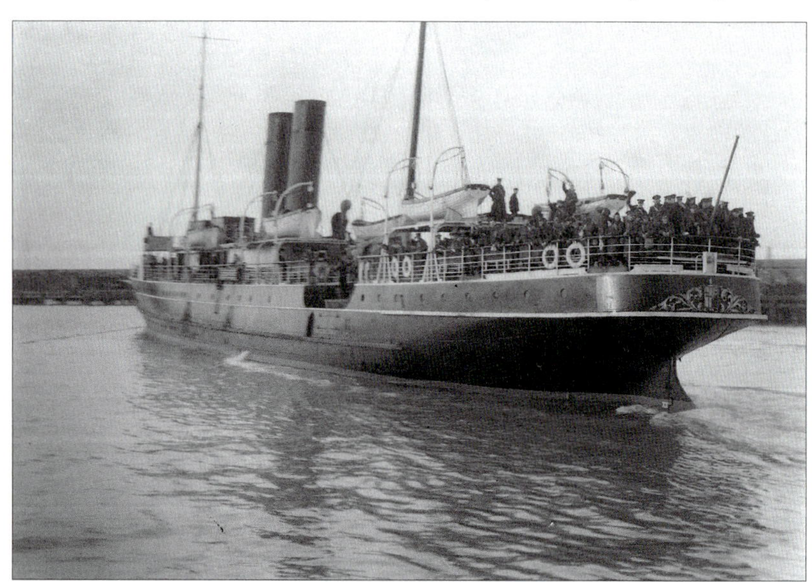

*Departure of the Jersey Militia Contingent from St Helier
Harbour on ship for service in the First World War (1915)*
SJPA/006025 Société Jersiaise Photographic Archive, Jersey

His name is Jurat Joshua George Falle, and he's king of this castle. Turns out his house is just as grand inside, with marble statues and velvet papered walls and great portraits of Advocates hanging beneath chandeliers. We whimper our names and confess our crimes. He nods, his eagle nose twitching, looking all smug. He spied us this time last Sunday, he smirks, and he's been waiting all week for his revenge.

Turns out Jurat Falle knows Walter's mother, so my mate got off lightly in the end. The Jurat dips his grand, gold-tipped fountain pen in a well of blue ink and writes a note for Walter to take home. His mother will read it and punish him at her own leisure. Strange to say, but I marvel at the copperplate font, the graceful swirl of the script. It's like a work of art. Poor Walt turns pale as a sheet, as if the Jurat has just handed out his death warrant. Tail between his legs, my friend scampers out the door.

"Well, I can't do the same thing to you, Tom Davis, for I do not know your parents." Why would he? Why would a man who hauled the nets and split the fish ever meet a man like this, unless he was on the other side of the dock? My mum Jemima wouldn't exactly bump into him either, unless she was clearing his laundry.

Cruel taskmaster that he is, the Jurat has another punishment in mind. He's going to make me clean all his boots, while he dines in silver-plate luxury, upstairs. He sends me down to the cellar, a dark and dusty basement beneath the house. Not as dingy as my home, mind, but definitely workers' quarters. Then he turns in the lock behind me and I am his prisoner, left alone with my chores.

So, I wipe off the mud and dirt, spit and polish the boots, and I am seething every moment with rage at my imprisonment. I still remember the look of those evil boots, as I scrubbed and scraped away in my anger. I left those shiny and clean Wellingtons arranged in military formation, as if they were the boots of a conquering army.

At last, the key turns once again, and my captor looms large in the door. "Well, Tom, now go home to your people. I hope that this punishment has been a lesson for you, and you will be a better boy in future."

He certainly wasn't expecting a reply. But I looked up and fixed that grand Jurat straight in the eye. I had nothing to lose, and I didn't feel afraid. I don't know how the words came to me like this, but they did, as if someone had written them down in a play and I was just reading out the script.

"One day, I will be a rich man. One day, I will stand at your door again. I will buy all of this from under you. And then I will tear your damned house down - stone by stone, brick by bloody brick. Mark my words, sir. This will come to pass."

Then I caught a strange look in his eyes, somewhere beneath his puffed-up indignation and the purple, bulging veins on his forehead. I sensed just the slightest quiver of fear.

*   *   *

Tom Davis
Ordinary Seaman, *Satellite* of Guernsey
February 1883

Shovelling coal isn't the best way to earn a fortune; but that's the life my father signed me up for. Soon enough, I was fourteen and my days in that dismal classroom at St Luke's Elementary School were drawing to an end. Chestnut thievery or no, my childhood days were done. So, I signed up as a deck boy on the *Alliance*, an old paddle steamer chopping down to St Malo. I was already nimble as a rat from my fishing days in my uncle's boat. The sea was where I belonged.

Like all crew-boys, I slept in the foc'sle, in the old 'donkey's breakfast', hopping with vermin and fleas. I loved every minute. The age of prattling old teachers and scolding Jurats seemed half a world away; I had now entered the world of men. This was the life I was born for; to run to the rhythm of the watch bells, to shinny up the rigging as if I was scaling the garden walls of Plaisance all over again.

It was sound enough work for seven shillings a week, but the French run was not enough. I was soon hungry for more. Then word came on the grapevine that Mr Allix, a Jersey shipmaster, was looking for seamen and coal haulers on the *Satellite*. This was a better prospect entirely, slicing up the British coast all the way to Shields, and bringing the black stuff home to Jersey. My heart leapt at the tantalising prospect of open seas and fresh horizons. My father had a quiet word with the captain and introduced me. The prize was in my grasp. So, I kissed my mother goodbye and signed the papers.

I was a few months shy of my sixteenth birthday when the voyage began. It was a shunting slow crawl at first, docking in pokey old St Peter Port and then cutting up the stubby Channel, past the chalk straits of Dover, until the swampy mouth of the Thames estuary opened up before us. We whisked past all those bleak flat marshes that I'd only read of in Dickens stories, where the fog rolls off the Saxon shore. Then we hauled up the narrowing river until the towers and spires of the capital finally hove into view.

Houses studded the hills and shoreline, growing ever thicker as Woolwich loomed before us. Soon enough we passed the serried armies of cranes, which flanked the East India Docks like sentinels along the river. The scales fell from my eyes as I drank in their sheer height. We passed the Isle of Dogs and I glimpsed the cavernous West India Docks for the first time. Any of those wharves could have swallowed up Quai des Marchands in St Helier for breakfast. My eyes bulged at those giant warehouses brimming with the fruit of Empire, spices from India and

Zanzibar, wool from New Zealand, and coals dragged from Newcastle. They're even hauling frozen meat and butter here from Sydney these days, right over from the far side of the world.

I suddenly realise the game we're up to. We are feeding the furnace, the factories whose fires light up the winter night, all the great arteries of the Empire clogged with fat and butter. Maybe one day too I can be part of this astonishing machine.

And beyond it all, I catch a glimpse of the ancient city of London itself, of the sun setting orange through the dirty ash clouds, through the pall of black coal-smoke that hung like a permanent shroud. I gaze towards the dirty dome of St Paul's, at the flocks of men swarming like pigeons, at the whirl of lights, at the dark brown river that slugs along beneath them. And I think of the gentleness and smallness of everything I have known.

We unload the cargo and after a back-breaking day where my spine aches like fire, we are rewarded with shore-leave. I am no drinker or gambler, so I observe it all with a watcher's eye. Men are lean and sharp here; they're dealers and traders, quick of wit and tongue, men with the gold-dust of ambition on their lips. I will have much to learn from them.

So, I heed all their stories: of sailing through the Golden Gate straits to San Francisco, of docking in the tropical paradise of Durban; of casting anchor in the great bay of Auckland. I slump back in my filthy straw mattress, my ears ringing with all the promises that lie ahead. I want it all.

But first of all, I'm going up to the coal docks of the Tyne.

*　　*　　*

The Satellite *shuffled east again, into the great grey estuary. This was the ship's habitual stomping ground, tracing the flat smudge of the Essex marshes. She skirted the rotting wooden pier at Southend and finally burst out into the German Ocean. The wind had risen, and they were pummelling up the English coast at great speed. The weather was fouling fast, spitting out great gobs of rain, and someone whispered that a gale was brewing. Night fell.*

During the morning watch, a funnel of cloud was seen racing in hard from the north, strangling the last clear patch of sunlight. The sky turned an ominous, petulant indigo. Then the forenoon bell rang and summoned Tom from four hours of kip on his flea-ridden mattress. He leapt into the ice-flecked breeze, reefing and trimming the sails, bringing the canvas in, fitting the Satellite *to ride out the storm. The ship rolled hard, and even hardened sailors felt a drawstring tighten in their guts.*

Tom could spy a smattering of church spires and the maw of Great Yarmouth;

they must already be far up the coast. The headwind grew snarling and vicious, bursting into an all-out storm, and the ship soon buckled before it. The skies turned black. And this is where the shallow sea grew traitor's teeth, baring a set of shoals. The coal-traders were skimming over the old Ice Age plain, a trove of axe-heads and mammoth bones. The hills of this drowned world had long since become great sandy ridges, lurking perilously just below the waterline. And with a shriek of pain, the Satellite foundered right up against one of them. "Ship aground!"

The 'Haisborough Sands' the old salts called them– or was it the 'Cross Sands'? The captain hastily rummaged through his charts, leery in his tilting cabin. Eight miles east of England; and stuck in thick mud. The shore lights winked teasingly across the void. Still, no harm done, he mused, just a simple mud-stuck embarrassment, and the tide will surely float us off when once the storm has spun itself out. Best be ready though, best be cautious: let us lower the longboat and put the Captain's chest aboard, lest the worst should happen. Who is the youngest, nimblest lad amongst us? "Tom Davis? Get to it, boy!"

Scrambling to the boat, Tom is loading it up now, a special task, a choice honour for the smallest boy on the ship. The longboat rolls violently but Tom deftly ties the chest down snugly. A single painter tethers the boat to its mother. Then the tide is pouring in around him hard, as fast as he remembers it from Jersey days. Suddenly it buoys up the Satellite, pushing it clean off the reef.

The painter slips. In the blink of an eye, the line whips back towards the ship, and is gone. The Satellite bucks up like a wild pony, cresting away on a surge of white foam, and is dragged in towards the shoreline. It is simply unable to turn. And Tom is soon hundreds of feet away, stranded in the longboat, watching the mother ship shrink to the size of a painted toy. He has been abandoned to the storm.

The Satellite will be snugly moored tonight in the Yarmouth Roads, reporting the regrettable loss of one soul, such a promising Jersey lad, not yet sixteen years of age. Far away, miles across the water, the longboat pitches over the waves. As the gale spews another violent cloudburst over it, a lone sailor gasps for breath and ballast.

Tom Davis is drifting over the deep, the plaything of the storm. He is many miles deep into the German Ocean, and utterly alone. The Jersey boy shivers on the open deck as the half-light bleeds away and the storm speeds on south. All is black now, and the night is drained of stars. He has no strength left to bail the boat.

Tom curls up like a drowned rat. In his feverish dreams, he is back in the choir-stalls at St Luke's, waiting for the sermon to end so he can scramble over the wall into paradise. They say it is a garden. Half-remembered words linger on feverish lips: "Lighten our darkness, we beseech thee, O Lord; and by thy great mercy defend us from all perils and dangers of this night...."

The wind sings its mockery, and the darkness abides.

*   *   *

The boy is dead, and words mean nothing any more. 'Young Davis of Georgetown', the Jersey press call him. Fifteen years old, his life cruelly snuffed out before it could ever blaze. Strange how the finest eulogies come from those who neither knew him nor cared. Mr Thomas Leopold Davis sits broken in his wooden chair, head cradled in his hands, as the last embers of the springtime storm fade over Jersey, and the priest comes to knock at the blackened door.

His son's memorial service will take place at St Luke's Church on Sunday morning. He has already agreed the readings and chosen the flowers, the cold white lilies of mourning. Canon Braithwaite offers a prayer and a comforting touch on the shoulder, then rides back alone to the churchyard. In the shadow of the church, a freshly dug grave-plot is waiting to be filled. Beyond the wall, on the other side, the gardens of Plaisance slumber. Jurat Falle's mansion looms large in the twilight like a ship's hull, bearing a string of lights on its stern.

The ship's lights are spelling out a name now: URDA. *In the old Norse, they say her name means Fate or Destiny; she is one of the Norns, the goddesses who decide the future of men. This one, though, is registered in Stavanger, and her job is carrying Norse oats to England. And as it punches through the storm, her crew notice a small, black longboat, floating past like driftwood on the tide. There is a boy at the helm.*

And the Norwegians winch him in, this poor drowned rat, hauling him safely over the wall. He must have spent nineteen hours or so at sea, caught in the eye of the storm, half-dead with shock. Perhaps this ship is named rightly after all. Deep in the bowels of the Urda, *Tom Davis slowly recovers his strength. A day later, he is dropped off with the cargo at Cowes, and an urgent telegram speeds across the Channel miles. The joyous news reaches his father on Saturday. The next day, his child comes home.*

The church service is about to begin. And as the congregation at St Luke's gathers in funeral black, the dead boy strides right up to the front of the church. Cheers erupt all around, and Tom beams at the faces of all those he loves and hates. Canon Braithwaite opens the service. "For this my son was dead, and is alive again; he was lost, and is found. And they began to celebrate".

*   *   *

T. B. Davis
Durban, South Africa
December 1939

After I was saved by the *Urda*, nothing in my life would ever be the same. The oceans unfurled before me like an open canvas of promise and opportunity. In the autumn of 1883, I stepped into the *Annie Fletcher* of Liverpool, and she showed me the world. We skirted the Devon coast and shot south like a cannonball, in a blinding run across the ocean towards the far side of the globe. The skies grew hotter and the sun scourged us until my neck peeled. My eyes blossomed with a sailor's squint and my clothes were soaked with sweat.

One day, we smashed clean through the Equator, through the burning girdle of the world. I was a newcomer to these parts, so the crew grabbed me from my bunk, and manhandled me up to the foredeck. There I was daubed with tar and soot, forced to down a seawater toast and offered up as a sworn sacrifice to old King Neptune. We finished the jolly proceedings with a tot of rum, and the southern seas shimmered around us like diamonds. Jersey was a distant, fog-bound memory. I was a man of the tribe now, a boy no more.

On and on; deeper and deeper. Through the mountain-waves of Cape Horn, where walls of water the size of Grosnez surged over us. We tracked the long and foreign shore of Chile, and finally docked in sultry Valparaiso. I joined yet another tramp ship, and ferried coal round the British coast. We came home to Jersey one morning, and that was the day my childhood finally ended. Without warning, my beloved mother keeled over, stricken by a late miscarriage. She was lying in the morgue by nightfall.

Two days later, I set sail again, and knew in my heart that this time I would never come home. The great voyages that follow are sharp as a pin in my mind's eye; from the coal-towns of the North to the sugar-towns of Barbados, and the cod-run from Oporto that ended in disaster. One of my berths, the *St Brelade* of Jersey, foundered and splintered in foul October weather on the Gaspé peninsula, but no mere shipwreck could slow me down now.

I prised this fine world open like an oyster. We made for San Francisco, the California boomtown where the streets flowed with gold back in the mad old days of '49. I remember the Golden Gate headlands shining, the mansions of Nob Hill and the gleaming cable cars spinning a web of beauty over the hills. Yet I stayed sober and strong during our nine-week layover, shunning the bottle and the bordello. Instead I stayed aloof, observing the ways and weaknesses of men, seeing how and when they stumbled. I watched the deals they made, the terms of trade, all their evasions and deceptions. I saw the same foibles and habits of men repeated again and again in Buenos Aires, in Port Said, in Nagasaki; the more I travelled, the more the world seemed to stay the same. I prayed daily and hard, as I had in the open, rain-lashed boat. I prayed for wisdom.

On shore leave in grimy old London, I fell in love. I had dared to study for an ambitious technical examination and had failed. I might be a born sailor, but the terrors of trigonometry tangled my mind. Yet nothing but the best is good enough; I was determined to wrest victory. I found a lovely lady tutor who came to my aid. My beloved Minnie was older than me, a widow with a child, a six-year-old boy who needed a father. We wed and soon I added another baby to the fold, Glenham, my son and heir. In the brick terraced streets of West Ham, he grew up strong. My buccaneering days on the sailboats were done. I needed a steady income. I joined the steamers.

Now I tramped the great sea highways of the British Empire; from Silvertown to Brisbane, down the Suez Canal to Aden and Ceylon and at long last to Queensland. We circled back via the New World, and I was on shore leave at Montevideo when I learned my second son had born. We called him Howard Leopold, and he was the light of my life.

I learned so much on these voyages. We ship out the finest industrial wares of the workshop of the world; we haul back meat and wool and honey from the colonies. Everything is weighed and counted and sorted, with fees earned and banked. Everyone takes a cut along the way, a margin lean or plump, and he who controls the machinery, who grasps the neck of the bottle, creams the fattest rewards. All these lessons simmered in my thoughts, waiting until the time was right.

Events forced me into it, dire events. Today I am a friend of kings, a wealthy man, a respected philanthropist, and yet that old accusation stings me like the schoolyard cane. I hit a man, they claimed; I brawled with the second officer. 'A most brutal assault', they wrote in my testimonial; and I was cashiered on the spot.

Back in the East End now, in the shadow of the workhouse, as my children brawl around me and my wife bitterly scolds me. I am almost a leper with the lines, my dismissal haunting me like a shadow, forced to cadge work where I can. At last I catch a lucky break; and find a berth on a tramping ship called the *Fernfield*. I would have scoffed at the pay a year ago, but now it seemed like manna from heaven.

We slingshot across the world, from America to Australia. Then we turn west across the immense blue reach of the Indian Ocean. This was the voyage that would change my world and set me on the course that would change my fortunes for good and for ever. I was first mate on a ship bound for the war fields, supplying the British Army on the front line. A ship bound for South Africa.

*   *   *

Some saw a country ripped apart by a bitter war, where the ports were stricken by plague and the mines had ground to a halt. I beheld only a vista of inexhaustible beauty and potential, a land of milk and honey. Port Natal was brimming with opportunity. '*Ex Africa semper aliquid novi*', as the master at St Luke's used to quote Pliny: 'Out of Africa, there is always something new'. This was the ideal place for a man like me, who had come from nothing, to build my fortune.

There could be no turning back. On 17th November 1900, aged thirty-three, I bought a one-way ticket on a steamship to Cape Town. I left Minnie and my three sons, including my new-born baby. I would leave my wife and sons behind to plot the course of my future, to take the helm of my life. As a failsafe, I bought a little cottage in Jersey, on Dicq Road, lest my plans come to naught. Best not to burn all bridges; my little altercation with the second officer had taught me that.

I need not have worried. Africa became my goldmine. I was thirty-three, in my prime, with markets to forge and a world to win. I took over a stevedoring business and it grew like a young elephant. I never mined a single ounce of gold or spun a bale of cotton myself; instead I ensured I controlled the pinch points, the neck of the bottle. I became a master wharfinger and stevedore, owning the docks and the lighters that loaded and unloaded the cargo. Everything that passed into Durban soon came through me, and I took a rich cut from every crate.

My baby son tragically fell victim to the London cholera epidemic, and after that blow, my wife and surviving children were ready enough to join me. On the far side of the world, in the eternal spring, we made a new beginning for ourselves.

The blessings flowed upon us like rain. In our opulent mansion on the Cowie Road, we soon welcomed two baby girls, healthy and strong. Business was tremendous. After all those years working myself to the bone for shillings on the shipping lines, I could scarcely believe how my hard work finally paid off. The stevedoring business began to yield unfathomable riches. Beyond East London and Port Natal, we expanded right along the Indian Ocean; into Beira and Mombasa. We swooped into Dar es Salaam as soon as the Germans shipped out. Now the lion's share of East Africa's trade passed through me. My long dark nights on the open ocean were over. Fate had smiled on me, something I mused on as I chose the telegraphic call-sign of my head office: URDA.

Then one day war came, and the trenches opened up like graves across the face of Europe. My boys, barely out of Michaelhouse, were swept up by battle-fever, eager for the fight. Glenham fought closer to home in southern Africa. Howard was on shore leave from his steamer in Glasgow when he heard the news that the

King had declared war. He raced to join up with the Highland Light Infantry, and soon enough was shipped out to Flanders. The hand of fear rested on my shoulder every day, in my sun-filled Durban office, as I read the newspaper dispatches from the wars. Glenham served with honour in Africa but was felled by dysentery and invalided out from the frontline.

On a Durban winter's morning came the blackest news of all. I took the telephone call and my world went cold. The sunlight, the palms, the glittering bay has become a mocking dream, and everything faded to black. Howard had fallen at Courcelette, a village on the Somme bought with much blood. My son lay seriously wounded now, in a field hospital. No-one could say if he would live or die. I remembered myself, lost on the open boat, praying in the night for rescue. I imagined the despair of my own father, when he heard I was lost, his rough voice cut straight from his lips, his body slumped, gutted like a fish. His grief had soon turned to mad joy, but I would be granted no such redemption.

A second telephone call. I already knew in my heart, long before I lifted the black receiver. I already knew.

*   *   *

The rest of my life is a mere footnote. I made further fortunes. I befriended the King of England, and we raced yachts together in the Solent. My own yacht, *Westward*, became a legend. Glenham took over my business. In my last few years, I started to give away the lion's share of my wealth, endowing my own flotilla of colleges and training ships. I tracked down the survivors of the *Urda*'s crew and distributed generous cheques. I established a new hall for Victoria College; funded an experimental farm; and provided a Jersey lifeboat. All was given in memory of the young man who haunted my dreams, my son who would never claim his inheritance.

Sometimes I sailed home to Jersey, and my grief always welled strongest here, whenever I walked the streets of my childhood home. Lost in an old man's thoughts, I ended up strolling past St Luke's, where the old house Plaisance still loomed over the churchyard. It taunted me from behind its wall, like an unsettling memory.

The fearsome old Jurat who had scolded me was long dead, and his daughter Lily Falle was an old lady now. She was keen to sell up and find somewhere smaller. So, I made a generous cash offer, explained my charitable plans for the estate, and I purchased it for the Island.

I looked at it one last time before I gave the final order, at those halls that had once held such terrors for me, now looking so shabby and small. I had once imagined this little provincial lawyer's house to be the greatest palace in the world. It meant nothing to me anymore.

The demolition men soon moved in. The great house was razed to the ground, struck from the pages of history. The grand wings and marbled foyer were replaced by smooth shadowed lawns, a delicate carpet of grass.

As I inspected the work, I observed they were simply sealing up the cellar where I had scrubbed the Jurat's boots. "Not good enough," I insisted. I wanted every inch of that wretched room torn out and destroyed, and the whole cellar filled up with earth, suffocated with rubble.

Brick by brick, stone by stone, my prophecy fulfilled. The little boy who uttered that mad oath had become a friend of kings, a millionaire many times over, the lord of a business empire that stretched thousands of miles across Africa. I had won the whole world, only to find that all the money on earth would never be enough, and it could not raise the dead.

*　　*　　*

I opened the park to the public in September 1939, as the guns of war began to thunder over Europe once again. I had a statue of King George V, my dear lamented friend, placed at the entrance. The flagpole next to it was a spinnaker boom from *Westward*, my favourite yacht, home at last. And the gates themselves bore the name of my lost son, my beloved son, Howard Davis.

Plaisance was gone. I left only the billiard hall standing, as a shrine, a Hall of Remembrance for my son and all of those we have lost. Around it the garden grows to this day, beautiful palms and banks of roses and trembling soft lawns. And when autumn comes, and the chestnuts fall, and the earth weeps, I will remember him.

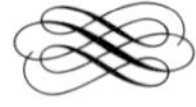

Red Letter Day: Sailing for War

*T*he sea carried away so many of Jersey's sons. Howard Davis was just one of hundreds of young men who would sail away to war, but never return. St Helier's harbour, now crowned by the New North Quay, had long been the crux of Island life, its vital gateway to the world beyond. This was where every journey began, and where every traveller came home.

These docks disgorged the finished goods of the Empire, bringing postal sacks and fresh crops of tourists down from the Southampton railhead. In return, the finest bounty of Jersey was marshalled here, packed and sent out into the world beyond.

In 1825 the first Weighbridge was built in front of the Southampton Hotel, designed to weigh and value potatoes and other produce. It became a hive of activity in the summer season, the pinch point through which each load must pass. The Jersey Railway built its terminus nearby, and when the upper harbour was filled, the Weighbridge was moved to a fine brick building closer to the water. With the burgeoning popularity of the Jersey Royal, the volume of potato exports became so great that extra arches soon had to be added.

The Weighbridge plaza was laid with elaborate gardens to mark the Jubilee, presided over by a statue of Queen Victoria herself. As the century closed and the evening shadows of her reign lengthened, Jersey basked in a somnolent and complacent peace. The warehouses along the Esplanade brimmed with potato sacks for export; the fruit of a prosperous century.

Yet Europe was soon to undergo a new weighing and judging, one that would determine the fate of nations. This time, it was the lives of Jerseymen which would be counted in the balance. At the New North Quay, it would be Jersey's own precious sons who would be gathered up for the harvest.

*   *   *

In the glorious May of 1913, Europe celebrated a lavish wedding. Princess Victoria Louise, the Kaiser's daughter, was getting married, and it was a splendid affair. Three doting cousins stood together; the King of England, the Emperor of Germany, and the Tsar of Russia. The meeting of these brotherly nations passed most amicably; Mayfair and County Society magazine enthused that 'the King and Queen's sojourn in Berlin has been remarkable proof of their popularity in the German capital'.

Just over a year later, the nations ruled by the three monarchs were locked in a brutal fight to the death. By the time the Great War ended, only one of those royal cousins still reigned. The second had fled for his life. The third had been ruthlessly executed by firing squad.

The idle reader of that same gossip magazine in 1913 would doubtless have also enjoyed the colourful portrait of a 'Man of the Day' closer to home, Sir William Henry Venables Vernon, Bailiff of Jersey. 'Jersey may well be proud of her Bailiff', opined the magazine, 'for there is no abler, no more energetic and progressive in every sphere of activity, no more deservedly popular man than he in the Channel Islands'.

As the new year of 1914 dawned, the Bailiff presided over an Island basking in economic prosperity and a thriving tourist industry. Yet even as holidaymakers settled into their deckchairs at Havre des Pas for what promised to be a splendid summer, the world they knew was spinning into the abyss.

On 28th June, Archduke Franz Ferdinand and his wife were shot dead in Sarajevo. Events soon acquired their own appalling momentum; like a chess game where moves could not be undone, where the fixed demands of treaty obligations and railway timetables determined the fate of millions.

On 28th July, Austria-Hungary declared war on Serbia. The German army was already massing on the Russian and French frontiers. Despite a flurry of desperate personal telegrams between Tsar and Kaiser, their bonds of kith and kin would not be enough to save them.

In snug and sleepy Jersey, on Wednesday 29th July, an astonishing notice was posted in the Evening Post *office window: after a century of peace, the Militia was being called to arms. The only world the people of Jersey had ever known, the endless summer of peace and prosperity, was drawing to a close. A long and bitter winter was at hand.*

That weekend, Europe stumbled like a drunken man into a ravine. On Saturday, Germany declared war on Russia. As Great Britain basked in its gorgeous Bank Holiday Monday, the Kaiser declared war on France. On the next day, the fourth of August, summer ended.

A Son's Story
The Jersey Company
March 2nd, 1915

This is the story of how I sailed from the New North Quay and became a man. The journey began at home; in the rocking chair by the fire, in our small family farm in rural St Helier. My father kicking over the coals with his hob-nailed boot, the waft of cabbage loaf from the oven; my baby sister wailing endlessly from the cot.

Every evening brought us news from 'The War': the thrilling nightly saga portrayed in the copies of the *Evening Post* my mother brought home. My eyes lit up at the headlines – the desperate struggle to stop the German advance as they cut through the French borderlands, punching west. For a few fretful weeks, we feared that the Kaiser's armies might soon be at the gates of St Malo.

Then came the miracle of Mons, when angels with longbows descended from heaven and saved the British Expeditionary Force in their moment of dire need. Next came the decisive battle of the Marne, when the entire fleet of Paris taxis was requisitioned to drive the French *poilus* to the front line, in a last ditch bid to stop the Kaiser's hordes. The line held. The tide turned. Perhaps this great clash of arms would be over by Christmas after all. We had not chosen to live in these dramatic times; but the times had chosen us. I longed to step into the heart of the story, to play my own part in this epic that would decide the fate of the world.

I had never cared much for our Jersey Militia training, for those dull freezing hours camped in deserted coastal watchtowers, all those tedious drill parades down at Greve d'Azette. It was a compulsory duty, a rite of necessity, shorn of glamour. What a cruel twist of fate to be stuck here on this rock, guarding our precious potato fields. And yet, my father still insisted he needed me for the harvest. The French farm workers had all been called up; we were short-handed enough as it was. I would sit sometimes on the rocks at La Collette and gaze out over the churning sea. Somewhere, far over there, the great guns were lighting up the Christmas sky, and empires were being won and lost.

We all heard the news, the first surreptitious announcements in the *Evening Post*. No longer would men have to travel to England to sign up to fight with strangers. Now they were raising a Jersey Company.

There was no escape from the call. I was at West's Picture House one night in the holiday season, when the film reel juddered to a crashing halt. Perhaps a fuse had blown? Then the limelight came on unexpectedly, and suddenly old Constable Pinel of St Helier hoisted himself on the stage. He was wearing his bright new chain of office, with the Jersey coat of arms hypnotically glinting at us in the stalls. The Constable squinted at the crowd, and there was fire in his eyes. Then he addressed us directly, speaking man to man. The war had come, he declared, and this was your time for choosing. "How would you wish to be remembered?" The time had now come for every true Jerseyman to do his duty. The call from the King was clarion clear, but how would we respond?

After another winter weekend spent with the Militia tramping the turnip fields, we passed by the barracks in Town. On the streets outside, a gaggle of coquettish, gorgeous girls were flirting with the boys. Their velvet plumage was soft as a bird's, their trilling, beautiful laughter came ringing after me down the street. They smiled at me. Then I suddenly caught their ice-white stares, the sneers hanging on their frozen lips. They were handing out white feathers. I turned away and ran, ashamed of my own shadow. Was I a coward, a snivelling little boy afraid of standing up to my own father? The very next morning, I reported for duty to my commanding officer.

When I came home to the farm, my parents already knew. My mother looked at me with such a glance, and tears welled up in her eyes. Then she embraced me. My father stared awhile into the fire, and at first, he said nothing. Then he put a strong hand on my shoulder. I would acquit myself well, he said. It would not be an easy path, but at the end of it all, I would become a man, and perhaps more than he had ever been. My little sisters, though, were not so easily consoled, and they wept together in my arms.

Nothing had changed, and yet everything had changed. We Volunteers were given red V sashes on the khaki; we were now deemed to be heroic, marked men. We were like the Roman gladiators of old, feted and feasted for a short while before we were sent to the heat and dust of the arena. Theatres laid on special gala performances for us; we toured schools; Constables and Jurats jostled to shake our hands.

Men whispered in admiration as we passed. Younger lads glanced at us with barely concealed envy. Well-to-do, prim girls threw us adoring, beatific smiles. And in the evening taverns of St Helier, freer young ladies drew us closer still.

*   *   *

We were proudly named the 'Jersey Company', attached to the Royal Irish Rifles. They said the regiment was having trouble recruiting, given the current turmoil in Ireland, so we would provide some welcome extra manpower. In our new Company, we would train, work and fight as a team. We carried the hopes and pride of the Island on our shoulders.

We proudly paraded before the great men of Jersey at Greve d'Azette barracks. The YMCA Camping Committee had decided to bestow us with a bevy of gifts. The Dean of Jersey spoke words of blessing over us: "You are going out from Jersey to fight this war, so that you may tell your grandchildren and possibly your great-grandchildren after them. You can tell them that you stood in the breach, that you decided to fight for the right. The people of Jersey are proud of you – proud that you have considered it your duty to go out and help keep back the foe". Jersey would never forget us, he promised, and one day soon, we would be assured of a great welcome home.

Then the YMCA's carefully curated gifts were solemnly distributed. I received a cigarette case with the Jersey coat of arms embossed on the front. There was a tinder cigarette lighter, and some soap in a packet, which will doubtless be very useful at the Front. There is even a stamped and addressed postcard that we can send back at any point, to request further supplies from home. Finally, we were presented with a copy of the New Testament, inscribed with a message from the late Lord Roberts, the famous Victorian hero, the victor of Lucknow and Abyssinia:

25th Aug 1914
I ask you to put your trust in God. He will watch over you and strengthen you.
You will find in this little Book guidance when you are in health, comfort when you are in sickness, and strength when you are in adversity.
Roberts.

As I read the scrawled dedication, my hair stood on end. I did not recognise the sensation, although I would come to know it well enough in time. It was not a pang of fear, rather a creeping and nameless dread.

For now, we basked in our halos, brothers in arms, bound with life and blood for a cause greater than ourselves. I had cousins, schoolfriends, family all around me, boys I knew from football and harvest, from church and from cider press. And we stood protected by the shield of the greatest Empire that the world had ever seen. Whatever terrors the Kaiser could unleash on us, I believed we would stand strong.

The day of departure was coming soon, and whispers spread like wildfire. Our chariot of fire would be docking, to ferry us over to Ireland for intensive military training. From there, fit to fight, we would travel on to meet our glorious destiny at the Front. Tomorrow would rise up and take us, and we would become men at last.

I had never left Jersey before. Within days, I knew I would have to say goodbye to my parents and my little sisters. I would be leaving behind everything that I had ever known. This was no childhood game of soldiers any more. How would I truly feel, as the ship slipped round Corbière, and Jersey became a distant smudge on the horizon?

At last the sealed orders were opened. The cheers echoed through the mess hall that evening and the men roared with joy. Reveille would be at a punishing hour, with breakfast at 05:00. We would muster in drill formation at the Royal Square at 06:00, and then we would march down to the docks. The great game had begun.

I spent my last night in Jersey, in the bosom of my sleeping Island. I lay there awake in my bed for hours, drenched with a surge of euphoria and fear, a strange and unexpected brew. Beyond the bare windows of the barracks, my future was waiting to claim me. I looked up and out at the web of stars, at the brightness beyond, and already I could see the flash of the guns.

A Mother's Story
New North Quay, St Helier
March 2nd, 1915

It was still dark when they gathered, and we stood there with them: the mothers, sisters and wives of our brave boys. In the murky, mist-shrouded morning, they stood in formation in Royal Square, standing ready for war. Despite the darkness of the hour, I could see their cleanly pressed khaki, their boots gleaming in the pale light.

They reported here for duty beneath the gilt equestrian statue of King George II, in this place where the Battle of Jersey had been fought and won. Here in the square where men had bled and died, our boys stood together on home soil for the last time. Under the wing of the States Assembly buildings, in the shadow of the Town Church, they gathered to serve.

"Are we downhearted?" shouted the onlookers. "No!" shouted back the brave lads. They were laden down with bread, jam, cheese and biscuits – a feast for the sea-voyage ahead. Ahead lay the training camps of County Cork, and beyond that, no man could tell.

The police had their hands full holding back the enthusiastic crowd, who cheered and roared with pride. Thousands of well-wishers were surging into the square now, and people mobbed on the Library steps to gain a better view – all crying, cheering, shouting, hailing the King.

I knew so many of these soldier boys – from school, from the farm, from family friends. Jimmy Scoones, the well-known St Helier footballer, could scarcely move as he was mobbed by his fans. We'd all read the tales of the magical truce last Christmas, when the guns fell silent and sworn foes knocked a ball around in no man's land, between the lines. His next match, he joked, will be against the Hun. And there was an ominous edge in his voice.

I spied my beloved son in the formation and made a hurried beeline for him. Our farewell was brief. Quickly, I stuffed some chocolate and a batch of Fry's cocoa into my son's backpack, and then I held him close for the last time. My little baby, now looking so strong and proud. Half-sheepish, half-elated, my boy kissed me on the cheek and then strode off jauntily to join his comrades, his brothers in arms.

Suddenly a crisp military bark echoed across the square and the soldiers –

Regular Army men now – stand to attention. Then the bugle band strikes up and leads them down Mulcaster Street, past the Town Church, all the way down to the quay. The Lieutenant-Governor and the Bailiff join old Lt Col Stocker at the head of the column, as he leads his Jersey boys down to the waterfront. Here, the SS *Ibex*, the chartered mail steamer, will be waiting for them.

Thousands of us had lined the Albert and Victoria quays in the early hours, all here to say goodbye to the men we loved. There were no barricades at the dockside to hold the crowds back; no-one was going to stop families from saying goodbye to their kin. Jersey was undivided as it released its sons for the great and fateful battle ahead.

High above us, the South Staffordshire Regiment stationed at Fort Regent manned the high ramparts in formation, cheering on the departing troops. Their roars echoed down over the harbour like rolling thunder, a deep-throated bellow of defiance. Down below, the soldier boys had broken into a lively chorus of *Tipperary* and whistled it all the way down to the quayside.

A cine-cameraman was cranking up his machine, turning the handle on history. He had been sent by West's Pictures to capture every detail of this momentous day, to bottle the lightning of this moment. No doubt the moving pictures of our children will be played over again and again at the picture-house in the coming weeks, sandwiched somewhere between the Keystone films and the latest Hollywood romances. It will prove a curious form of immortality.

The assembled potentates of Crown, church and law stood ready to greet the soldiers as they ascended into the bowels of the ship. First to welcome them was the Lieutenant-Governor himself, the illustrious Brigadier-General J.W. Godfray. Then the Dean of Jersey gave his blessing for their glorious undertaking. Finally, the Bailiff, William Venables Vernon himself, bade them farewell.

The grand old dignitaries shook hands with each and every soldier. "Truth be told, we heartily wish we could go with you, if only the call of duty did not detain us." I was not so sure. We knew these great men were destined to die snug and old in their beds, tucked far away from the machine gun bullets, or the exploding artillery shells, or the dread whisper of poison gas.

We had only caught glimpses of the Front from the veiled press reports, but we were no fools. We shed a tear when our friends drew their curtains at noon and changed into black. We read the advertisements for 'Mourning Suits' that had started to spring up in the press. And now there would be nothing to keep our sons safe but our prayers.

At the very end, the brass band struck up into a stirring rendition of *Long Live the King*. Two by two, our boys walked up the gangway, like the toy animals boarding the Ark in Sunday School. Those days seemed only yesterday, and now this was their childhood's end.

Around me, I beheld a picture from a strange and distant dream. The tide was high in the harbour. The sea all around was as smooth as glass now, as flat as a mill-pond. The Jersey flag fluttered limply around on every side, on the Commercial Buildings, on the *Duke of Normandy* tug, from the masts of every sailing boat frozen in the harbour.

They were still doling out last rations of cigarettes as farewell offerings to each one of the soldiers as they stepped up to board. This was their generation's adventure, their calling. We were left behind, relics of an older world that no longer mattered, and we could never understand.

As the very last Jersey Volunteer boarded, the gangway hatch was sealed. Then the band broke out into the haunting melody of *Auld Lang Syne*. The mood of the crowd turned in a moment, and as we mouthed the words, a terrible wave of tears broke over us all. I was weeping unashamedly now, and my shawl was soaked by my tears. I could still see my son's face there above the railings, where he was jammed like a sardine, smiling and waving at me. Forever smiling.

Then the moorings were silently slipped and the mailboat pushed away. The waters parted before them. Even as they drifted further and further away, the hearty cheers from the deck floated over the water, dwindling only with the horizon. They already sounded like voices from a vanished world. Our children were gone.

The astonishing theatre had reached its crescendo, and the curtain was coming down. The Army had brought a signalling cannon down to the pierhead, and it thundered several volleys as the SS *Ibex* passed it. Perhaps the next cannon those boys would hear would be on the Western Front.

The SS *Ibex* steamed out west, away from the dawn, along the bosom of St Aubin's Bay. I hurried over to the Esplanade to catch a clearer view of its departure.

Suddenly the rising sun burst out from the clouds, and an angel of light danced across the harbour. A good omen, the papers would call it. And there the ship stood once again, a black silhouette against the gleaming horizon. Then the shadow passed over, beyond Noirmont Point, and slid into history.

A wisp of black smoke lingers for a moment, curling up into the winter skies. Then the horizon is empty. The smiling baby that had nestled in my arms, the young lad who had shinnied up the pear trees in the orchard; the sulky youth who had downed cider in their shade: all of them have left me now. My boy has gone.

Back home, all seems deceptively and mockingly unchanged; the orange coals in the grate, the old farm-dog curling at our feet, the bare trees in the orchard, their black arms holding out for Spring. I read the crisp black banner in the *Evening Post*, read in the flickering gas-light: 'The Proudest Day in Our History'. The tributes are fulsome: 'Enthusiastic scenes on the quay'. A 'Red Letter Day', the papers are calling it. This morning has already passed into the chronicles of history.

My boy's name is listed there in the paper tonight, standing proud amongst the roll-call of brave young warriors. I only pray that their names will not soon enough be carved in granite. My husband has nothing more to say. He knocks the tobacco out his pipe and shuffles off to bed.

This evening, in the silence of my room, I light a candle for my son.

*　　*　　*

The Jersey Company spent a summer of military training in the idyllic countryside of County Cork, and then transferred to muddy Aldershot for their final battle preparations. With Guernsey troops based nearby, the young troops found the opportunity for a final Muratti-style football match with their neighbours. On 23rd October 1915, Jersey celebrated a convincing one-nil victory over their sister Channel Island.

Yet these happy days could not last forever. Winter was coming. With the British Army suffering appalling casualties, fresh blood was urgently needed. Fortified by a final round of 'Christmas gifts' sent by their countrymen – cakes, pipes, apples and notepapers – the soldiers prepared for their final deployment. The trains led them straight to Southampton Docks, but they would not be taking the steamship home to the hearths of St Helier. Instead, they were bound straight for the War.

On the fearsome winter's night of New Year's Eve, 1915, as one bloody year of carnage ended and a still bloodier one began, the Jersey Company took up their posts in the trenches, manning the firing line. The glorious illusions of youth were stripped away in a moment. The Jerseymen had arrived at the gates of hell.

Europe had been ripped open by the war. The twin parallel snakes of the trenches stretched 440 miles from the Channel coast to the Swiss mountains. This was a brutal, mechanised war, unlike any in history, fought through the yellow-green burning fog of mustard gas, employing the terrifying innovations of aerial warfare and battle tanks, and yet bogged down in a seemingly intractable stalemate.

Some observers even feared that the war was less of a series of events, more a terrifying new creation: a fearsome industrial machine that could only be fuelled by human sacrifice. Perhaps the war would never end, becoming, rather like the aeroplane or motor car, a permanent feature of the modern world. As the cultural historian Paul Fussell later observed, the shocking proximity of this mad slaughterhouse to the safe and comforting world of home was a source of profound irony. Exquisite hampers from the refined London halls of Fortnum & Mason could be posted straight to their grateful recipients in the lice-ridden, medieval squalor of the trenches.

Prime Minister Lloyd George, asleep in Downing Street, would be jolted awake in 1917 by the seismic impact of the explosions hundreds of miles away at the Messines ridge. The shellfire of the trenches was regularly heard in the holiday resorts of the south coast of England. Jersey nestled a little further away from the Front yet was hardly unscathed. A large new prisoner-of-war camp mushroomed at Blanches Banques in St Ouen and it was soon filled with hundreds of captured German soldiers. The war ground relentlessly on. The black rain of telegrams from the War Office plunged family after family into grief, and the Jersey newspapers overflowed with obituaries and advertisements for funeral clothes.

The grand Victorian dreams of universal progress and human peace – the spirit that had motivated the Great Exhibition in the far-off days of 1851 – had come to naught. In this gleaming new twentieth century, thousands of young men would die to secure a few yards of empty mud.

The Jersey Company would be tested with fire throughout the pivotal year of 1916. The boys were first committed to the front line in the coal-country of Loos. At first, they were smothered by the blizzards of the northern French winter. Then, as the snows melted and the April rains lashed down, they succumbed to an epidemic of trench foot. The losses began to mount. Snipers and sepsis struck alike without mercy, and the list of dead and wounded lengthened. Captain Johnson, second in command of the Jersey Company, was blown up by an artillery shell.

The brave and committed Major Stocker, at age forty-nine, proved to be too long in the tooth for the rigours of trench warfare. He was felled by pneumonia and sent to England to recuperate. Over in France, his boys continued to die. Then came the shock news – the Jersey Company were needed for the greatest offensive in military history. They were being transferred to the Somme.

*　　*　　*

Men continued to die on land and sea. 1916 witnessed the epic sea battle of Jutland; the largest naval engagement the world has ever seen. In the grey North Sea, the two greatest navies in the world met in a titanic clash of arms. A number of Jerseymen experienced this defining moment in maritime history, and one played a critical role in the battle. For the commander of the Royal Navy's 1st Battle Squadron was Vice Admiral Sir Cecil Burney, born in St Saviour's Parish.

His flagship HMS Marlborough *was amongst the first to engage the Imperial German Navy but was grievously wounded by a direct hit from a torpedo. Contemporary accounts describe his ship as being lifted out of the sea, as if it were a rubber ball. She kept in the battle line for as long as she could, but water was relentlessly flooding in. Eventually, Vice Admiral Burney was forced to transfer to a new flagship, and HMS* Marlborough *limped back to the Humber.*

The ship's bruised return seemed an appropriate metaphor for an epic but frustratingly indecisive encounter. British public opinion considered Jutland to be something of a poor show, set against the inflated expectation of a crushing Nelsonian victory. Yet the German High Seas Fleet would never dare to directly confront the Royal Navy again, and some believe that in those days of blood and fire at Jutland, the war was truly won.

Yet the losses accumulated, and Jersey continued to count its dead. Vernon Williams, the Bailiff of Jersey who had greeted the troops as they disembarked, remained in office as the calamity of the Somme unfolded and the Jersey Company met its eventual fate in the heroic struggles for Guillemont and Ginchy. He watched as the Kaiser's strength began to buckle, and as victory appeared as a tantalizing beacon on the horizon.

As the stalemate of the trenches exploded into the dramatic land battles of 1918, the popular mood in Jersey turned. 'Now is the time to put every ounce of energy and every penny into the War. It is nearing the turning point', screamed the adverts for War Bonds in the Evening Post. *The end came just as Jersey emerged from a virulent spasm of Spanish flu. West's Picture House and other public venues had closed; the States Sanitary Committee was begging for volunteers and motor vehicles to deliver medicines to the rural parishes ('petrol will be provided'). The Hospital made an emergency appeal for nurses.*

Then the joyful news broke: 'Armistice Signed: God Save the King'. The signal post at Fort Regent was decked in bunting. Four ex-Tommies, each missing a leg, paraded through St Helier draped in flags and sang joyous songs with the crowd. Peace had been restored, yet the world of 1914 could never return.

The war had seemingly changed nothing in Jersey, and yet it had altered everything. Jersey's granite heart had fractured, and the wound would never heal. If all the British Empire's dead marched abreast past the Whitehall Cenotaph, they said, it would take three and a half days for the parade to pass by. Jersey's death toll per head of population had been among the highest of all.

A quarter of the Jersey Company were dead. The survivors were sent to occupy the Rhineland until 1919 and were only demobilised in dribs and drabs as the year wore on. One by one, the New North Quay received back its sons. There was no pomp and fanfare to mark their homecoming. So many returned as maimed men. In their heads, they heard the echoes of shellfire that would ring for decades; some carried splinters of metal buried deep within them.

The Jersey soldiers had won a war, but the sunlit uplands they longed for proved a cruel illusion. Bread and butter frustrations mounted, and the simmering tensions erupted during the General Strike of 1926. St Helier's harbour was caught up in this national convulsion, and the Jersey dockers refused to unload any cargo that had been handled by strikebreaking labour. Perishable food threatened to rot in the ships, and volunteers had to step in to help.

As Jersey slid into the ominous shadows of the Thirties, it could not escape the unfinished legacy of the Great War. The maelstrom had dredged up an aimless, bitter housepainter from Vienna and given him his beloved 'Front' experience; now Hitler would exploit the grievances of defeat to bully Europe. This time, the war would not stay confined to some faraway battlefield. In a few cataclysmic weeks in 1940, the Wehrmacht achieved the prize that had eluded it in 1914 and 1918: a knock-out blow on the Western Front.

The tables of history had swiftly turned, and the settled verdict of the Great War was hastily being rewritten. On June 22nd, in the same railway carriage in Compiègne where Germany had signed the 1918 armistice, Hitler accepted the surrender of France. Fortune's wheel had, it seemed, come full circle.

One of the bedraggled German prisoners-of-war held at Blanches Banques in St Ouen all those years ago had been a young lad called Erich Gussek. Over two decades later, in the summer of 1940, he would return to Jersey. This time he would come to the Island not as its prisoner, but as its overlord.

He was the first Kommandant of the German Occupation.

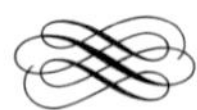

Epilogue: Flight of the *Ragamuffin*

Diary of a Jerseyman
August 1941

This is how the world falls into shadow. If you close your eyes, it is almost possible to imagine that nothing has changed this past year. The glorious sun still shines over our Jersey côtils, and the waves still lap beautifully on our freshly mined beaches. Try to ignore the swastikas, the eagles and the great grey guns. Try and forget the dull ache deep in our bellies, as we grow thinner by the day.

At first, there were just months of endless waiting. The war caught us all by surprise, like a rainstorm on a summer's day. Brothers, fathers, sons signed up and left for the fight, as they had done a quarter of a century past. Then little happened. We revelled in this long and phoney interlude, this time when nothing changed, when holidaymakers still booked summer breaks here, far from any danger. The Western Front was some faraway place, of towers and fortifications and concrete walls. We had seen this story before.

Then the Front collapsed. The German Panzers sliced through France like a knife through Jersey butter. This was the decisive victory that the Kaiser's armies had failed to achieve in four years at the cost of millions of lives, and now Hitler had done it in six weeks. The world reeled with shock.

We knew it was over now, and the Nazis would be coming for us soon. On Sunday 9th June, the day the French government evacuated Paris, a black funnel of smoke covered the whole sky. It hung over the Island for hours, billowing and acrid, like a terrible omen. I suppose it must have been a petrol supply dump in France, torched during the final retreat. That Wednesday, Paris was declared an open city. Then, on Friday 14th June 1940, the German Panzer divisions marched straight into the City of Light. France had fallen.

The shadow deepens. British soldiers begin to land in Jersey, disconsolate and sombre, a waymark on their journey home. A little Jersey flotilla heads down to St Malo, including pleasure boats sent from the St Helier Yacht Club. They are braving their lives to rescue British troops, to snatch just a few more from the maw of the approaching beast.

The soldiers are grateful at their deliverance, but they will not be staying here to fight for us. Fear sweeps the Island. There's a run on the banks; no money to be had. There's panic buying in the stores. Shelves begin to empty. We know that Cherbourg, just across the water, has already fallen. Then comes the official confirmation of what we've dreaded. Jersey has been demilitarised. It will not be defended. All who wish to leave must do so at once.

There are frenzied scenes in the harbour as the evacuation ships depart. Desperate families splinter and break. By Friday 21st June, all of them are gone; the Lieutenant-Governor, the soldiers, the evacuees, everyone. Some families even flee in the middle of a meal, leaving their homes unguarded, their furniture and everything they knew behind them. Better to lose everything than to live under the Nazi yoke, they must have reckoned. The last civilian aeroplane leaves the Airport that afternoon, a black speck receding in the summer sky. We who remain, must stand alone.

A week later, Jersey explodes. Three German aeroplanes swoop in without warning on Friday 28th, coming in from La Rocque, machine-guns firing. They drop a brace of bombs on the Weighbridge and the harbour, killing and maiming as they pass over; a vicious warning shot. The Pomme d'Or, the Royal Yacht and the Commercial Buildings are hit; even the furze on Fort Regent is set ablaze. Then there's an eerie pause, and instead of bombs they simply drop leaflets, calling on us to surrender. That's the end of the game. It is over.

And a year later, here we are; this is sunny Jersey in the summer of 1941. Behind the lingering traces of the holiday camps, the old façade of normality, we are living as if hollowed out and raw. The States still meet with all the pomp and ceremony of the ages, but they operate under the eyes of the German military command. The shops are still open, but they are practically bare.

We must all drive on the right now; we have to run on Central European Time. This Island has been welded into the machine of the Reich, the outermost flank of the continent of blood and iron. Gradually, Jersey is being changed. The Airport runway has already been extended, with the old barracks and farms demolished to make way for the needs of the war machine. There are rumours that much worse will follow. They say we have more soldiers per square mile here than in Germany.

There are now three layers of police authority here; the honorary police, the States of Jersey police and the German military police. Their firing squad is our highest court of law. When some poor brave French boys landed in Guernsey, one of them was taken to St Ouen's Manor and brutally executed.

I seethe with bitter anger at the Occupation, but I find it hard to hate the individual occupiers. Most are young boys just like us, caught in the grip of a machine beyond their imagining. They are themselves treated with brutal discipline, like mules. We are all caught up together in this infernal device. We are all puppets in the show.

In truth, our darkest fears have not yet been realised. Some even suspect the

Nazis wish to kill us by a pretence of kindness, to turn us into some kind of sick propaganda show for their twisted regime. It is true there are no mass graves or death squads here; our womenfolk walk unmolested; and we are not even shoved off the pavement when the stormtroopers goose-step down King Street. Perhaps we should be grateful for these small mercies.

In name only, the States continues about its business. But we bear only the fig leaf of freedom. The swastika flies over Mont Orgueil. The picture house is forced to show awful anti-Semitic propaganda. And we are slowly beginning to starve.

Within two weeks of the Germans arriving, the shelves of our shops were empty. The rationing is unremitting: two ounces of butter a week; two ounces of sugar, and four and a half pounds of bread for a man. There is no soap left here anymore. We are being slowly forced back into foraging, back to a more primitive way of life. We make coffee from baked parsnips and stir blackberry leaves to make tea. Even our clothes are falling apart, and whenever a shoe breaks, we nail on a wooden sole.

The weight is falling off people, giving them a false sheen of health at first, that soon turns sickeningly sour, until ribs poke out from under stretched skin and we end each day weak and lethargic. We give our children as much food as we can spare. Slowly, we are all becoming wan and ghostly. The tailors have never been so busy, taking in clothes. Gradually we are all becoming shadows of our old selves.

Thanks to the black market, though, some of the rich still thrive. A hundred pounds sterling will buy you a brimming sack of sugar. A scrawny pony that used to fetch twelve pounds is now snapped up for eighty. They might as well be selling a unicorn, for all that the common man can still afford to buy one. The poor have always been with us, and now most of us have been thrust into their ranks.

Electricity is rationed. Petrol is hoarded jealously, like liquid gold. The States members always seem to have enough; doctors are allowed a meagre ration. Farmers do not receive enough fuel for motorised ploughing; so, horses are kings of the land again. We have to make do with bicycles to move around. It is as if we are being pulled back into the nineteenth century.

All around us, part of the furniture now, are seven thousand or so German soldiers, young and handsome men, smiling, chatting and joking. Compared to the milling machine of the *Ostfront*, they must feel they are living in some kind of paradise. The officers lounge in the lobby of the Pomme d'Or, enjoying a smoke, savouring their days in the sun.

And in the East, it seems that history is advancing towards its long-awaited end. The Germans are smashing deep into the heartland of Russia, and the press dutifully recounts their roster of victories. Russian names, places we have scarcely heard of, seem to be falling like ninepins. The picture-houses show smiling young men, blond and bold, advancing deep into the breadbasket of Russia. Is it truth or lies, propaganda or fact? We can scarcely tell.

Jersey, it seems, has been struck off from the order of men. We are preserved in this strange and oppressive goldfish bowl, while the whole world burns around us. We imagine what must be happening on the mainland, the bombs falling on those we know and love. The cathedral cities of England must now be burning cauldrons. Whenever the RAF targets the port of Brest, we can feel our own doors and windows rattle. Flames lick the eastern skies over the Cotentin peninsula, and we know the war must still be going on, that the struggle is far from over. There is still a strand of hope remaining in Pandora's box, however threadbare it seems.

And in tiny imprisoned Jersey the Centeniers still keep order, and the parish churches gather every Sunday, as they always have done. We are even permitted to pray for King and Commonwealth, a surprising concession from a regime that would destroy both. The States still meet dutifully, with the pomp of the ages, enjoying a charming parody of freedom. But we are strangers in our own land now. We walk the same roads and streets we always have done, but they are no longer ours. Jersey has slipped into darkness.

*　*　*

Ragamuffin, The English Channel
September 1941

A boat is gliding north in the autumn night. It is a tiny open craft, a speck of driftwood in the cold, grey Channel, and tonight it bears a lean and thirsty young man. This is no ordinary craft. The *Ragamuffin* is one man's deliverance from a living nightmare, the German Occupation.

Denis Vibert has tried to escape once before. He was twenty-two, in the prime of his strength, and had trained as a merchant navy cadet. For some, hope was smothered, or broken. Denis believed there was still a way out. He burned with frustration and rage as swastikas were draped over the Island, as the conquering German soldiers strutted down King Street. He raged silently as Jewish residents were asked to register, as his food rations dwindled. Like so many Jerseymen, he longed to play his part in the war, to fight against his captors. Yet on a tiny, incarcerated Island, overt resistance would only end with a bullet.

So, he decided, in 1940, to break out of his prison and join the British forces. The attempt almost cost him his life. He endured four days of storms and sickness, clinging to the Roches Douvres reef, desperate for a break in the weather. At the end, his boat was wrecked on the rocks, and he had to swim a freezing quarter-mile to shore. Thank God, his absence had not been discovered. Most would have lost heart, learned their lesson, and grudgingly knuckled under the yoke. Not this man.

He was determined to try again. He hid a tiny eight-foot boat at his house – illegally, of course. It was called *Ragamuffin,* a name fit for a little rebel, a defiant rascal. He concealed two little outboard motors nearby. He siphoned petrol from a German lorry, a crime which the German Field Police would have punished with the utmost severity. With the help of friends, his boat was smuggled to the beach.

It was September of 1941, harvest time. This September, the potato crop had been replaced by barley and oats, the food of survival, and the tractors had no fuel. The men worked in the fields, like their grandfathers, with heavy horse-drawn ploughs. The setting sun dipped over Jersey, lighting up the blood-red swastikas on the town hall, the gunmetal-grey Luftwaffe aircraft taxiing at the airport, and the ancient fields. The sky burned like a candle over St Ouen's Bay, and then the sun slipped into the folds of the ocean.

Night fell like a shroud over a seething continent. In the west, the swastika fluttered over the Eiffel Tower. On the eastern edge of the Reich, German artillery moved within close shelling range of Leningrad. The final collapse of the Soviet Union appeared imminent. Already, the Kiev pocket was imploding, and by month's end its surrender would yield half a million Russian prisoners. That September night, Europe slept to the endless dance of the searchlights and the orange flare of high explosives, of cities slowly burning.

In occupied Jersey, Denis headed down to the silent beach at Bel Royal, where his little *Ragamuffin* was waiting for him. The night was starless, and the German sentries did not see him. Now was the hour to make his bid for freedom. He burst out quickly into St Aubin's Bay, and was soon making good headway. The lights of the Harbour glistened over the dark water. His past life, his friends, his home were left behind; but he had made his choice. He would fight.

Four miles out, disaster struck. A pair of German E-boats on secret manoeuvres slipped by him in the dead of night. Hulking and brutal craft, they were travelling at high speed. Thank God, the night patrol did not see him, but the violent force of their wake almost turned him over. His boat rocked and stabilised, but he was drenched, and his food supplies were utterly ruined. His outboard engine too, was left waterlogged and useless. Gingerly he unwrapped his remaining lifeline; his spare engine. Yet as he leant to fix it on, another surge struck; his fingers fumbled, and the engine sank like hope, like a dying prince, beneath the waves. There was nothing for it. His oars alone would have to carry him to England.

So, he began to row like a madman, desperately pulling through a hundred tortuous miles of open sea. Though the grey English Channel, the funnel of sea where the White Ship foundered, where generations of Jerseymen sailed west to Newfoundland, where RMS *Titanic* had steamed out from Southampton only twenty-nine years before. Across this thin grey sleeve of sea, the flooded Channel valleys, the mere accident of geography that had saved the mainland from the same fate as the Islands.

The last of his water supply had now gone. Like Louisa Journeaux during her ordeal, he had nothing left to sustain him but hope. Three days and nights on the open sea, without sustenance, straining and tormented, he was driven half-frenzied with sweat and thirst. His arms were raging and torn, his hands bruised and bloated from the rowing. Yet he would go on, and Jersey would go on, because in the end there was no other way.

Through the darkest hours, through the terrors of the night. He was rowing for those left behind, those still trapped in the darkness and yearning for freedom. The gulls were screeching and wheeling high above him, as if they were free men, as if they already knew.

Denis rowed on into the first light. And then at last, dawn broke. Portland Bill was rising up to meet him, and the grey hull of the King's ship, HMS *Brocklesby*, was drawing up beside him, like an angel of liberty, bringing him safely in.

Liberation would come to Jersey at the appointed time; that much he knew. As he collapsed into blissful sleep, he thought he could still hear the voices of all those he had left behind, pacing down the watches of the night, praying in the darkness, waiting for morning.

THE END

Acknowledgements

Above all, loving thanks are due to my wife and my family, who allowed me to spend so many weekends researching and writing this book, and also to my parents, who encouraged my early love of writing.

I am grateful to Graham for introducing me to Philip Ahier's classic work, *Jersey Sea Stories*, and for suggesting the unifying theme of maritime history.

I would also like to thank Dawn for her feedback, and of course Roger Jones, my unfailingly supportive publisher at Seaflower Books.

This book is in loving memory of my grandfather Ronald, who served in the Royal Navy from 1931 to 1946, and my grandmother Joan, who served in the Women's Royal Naval Service from 1943 to 1946.

About the Author

Paul Darroch is a former Centenary Scholar at St Hugh's College, Oxford and is the author of *Jersey: The Hidden Histories* (Seaflower Books, 2015). His website is www. historyislands.com and he can be found @HistoryIslands on social media.

Complete list of Seaflower Books 2019:

BLAME THE BADGER by Mike Stentiford OBE	£6.95
CHANNEL FISH by Marguerite Paul	£11.95
CHEERS! Drinks & drinking in Jersey through the ages by Alasdair Crosby	£9.95
EXOTIC GARDEN PLANTS IN THE CHANNEL ISLANDS by Janine Le Pivert	£9.95
A FARMER'S VACATION IN 1873 by George E Waring	£5.00
GUERNSEY COUNTRY DIARY by Nigel Jee	£4.95
ISLAND DESTINY by Richard Le Tissier	£6.95
ISLAND KITCHEN by Marguerite Paul	£12.95
JERSEY IN LONDON by Brian Ahier Read	£6.95
JERSEY JAUNTS by John Le Dain	£5.95
THE JERSEY LILY by Sonia Hillsdon	£5.95
JERSEY: NOT QUITE BRITISH by David Le Feuvre	£6.95
JERSEY OCCUPATION DIARY by Nan Le Ruez	£9.95
JERSEY RAMBLES by John Le Dain	£6.95
JERSEY: THE HIDDEN HISTORIES by Paul Darroch	£9.95
JERSEY WAR WALKS by Ian Ronayne	£8.95
JERSEY WITCHES, GHOSTS & TRADITIONS by by Sonia Hillsdon	£6.95
JOURNEY ROUND ST HELIER by Robin Pittman	£7.95
LIFE ON SARK by Jennifer Cochrane	£5.95
MINED WHERE YOU WALK by Richard Le Tissier	£6.95
PROMISES NOT FORGOTTEN by Gerald Breen	£11.95
THE POOR SHALL INHERIT Daff Noel	£6.95
WILD ISLAND by Peter Double	£7.95
WILDLIFE OF THE CHANNEL ISLANDS by Sue Daly	£14.95
WISH YOU WERE HERE by John Le Dain	£7.95

Please visit our website for more details: **www.ex-librisbooks.co.uk**
SEAFLOWER BOOKS may be ordered through our website using Paypal
We send books post-free within the UK and Channel Islands
SEAFLOWER BOOKS are also available via your local bookshop or from Amazon.com

SEAFLOWER BOOKS

11 Regents Place, Bradford on Avon, Wiltshire, BA15 1ED
Tel/Fax 01225 865191   e-mail: roger.jones@ex-librisbooks.co.uk
www.ex-librisbooks.co.uk